"Dr. George Yancey argues that the two paths of colorblindness and antiracism have not worked and will not work to solve the country's problems and heal its pain resulting from a racialized society. Dr. Yancey contends that the path of colorblindness ignores racialized problems, and the path of antiracism causes a racially hostile society to be even more hostile and polarized instead of bringing ethnically diverse people together. Dr. Yancey argues for a third path that he calls 'mutual accountability/responsibility' or 'collaborative conversations.' This approach invites ethnically diverse image-bearers to be proactive and take personal responsibility to enter into collaborative conversations with the intent of working together with all ethnically diverse image bearers of goodwill to solve racialized problems. For those interested in getting off the paths of colorblindness and antiracism, Dr. Yancey's book offers a third path to help God's image bearers get closer to the promised land of both racial healing and a racially fair society."

Jarvis J. Williams, associate professor of New Testament interpretation at the Southern Baptist Theological Seminary

"There is not a more theologically sound, empirically informed, well-reasoned, or rational voice addressing the complexities of race, class, and culture in America today than that of Dr. George Yancey. In *Beyond Racial Division*, he navigates nuance and effectively challenges readers to get beyond rhetoric to results in their engagement of diverse others. As did Christ with arms outstretched, Yancey herein seeks to unite motivations and to hold Christ-followers in tension so that we might walk a more productive path for the sake of the gospel, and in so doing lead others away from painful polarization, beyond the crippling distinctions of this world that otherwise divide."

Mark DeYmaz, cofounder, president, and CEO of the Mosaix Global Network, author of *Building a Healthy Multi-Ethnic Church*

"Our racial division and inequality are extreme. In the midst of such challenges, we shout, we accuse, we point fingers, we divide into camps. And we get nowhere. Dr. Yancey proposes an alternative, rooted deeply in Christian understanding and sociological knowledge. He offers hope and clarity for our times. A must-read."

Michael O. Emerson, professor and head of the sociology department at the University of Illinois Chicago and coauthor of *Divided by Faith: Evangelical Religion and the Problem of Race in America*

"Race relations in the United States are mired in acrimony, tribalism, and polarization. What is really needed as a key first step is the pursuit of better listening to one another. Yancey's *Beyond Racial Division* is a sensitive and sane proposal for how to go there while assessing current options with care and balance. It presents a distinctive third way. If you read one book on issues tied to race, this is it."

Darrell L. Bock, executive director for cultural engagement at the Hendricks Center for Christian Leadership and Cultural Engagement, senior research professor of New Testament studies, Dallas Theological Seminary

GEORGE YANCEY

BEYOND
RACIAL
DIVISION

**A UNIFYING
ALTERNATIVE TO
COLORBLINDNESS
AND ANTIRACISM**

An imprint of InterVarsity Press
Downers Grove, Illinois

InterVarsity Press
P.O. Box 1400, Downers Grove, IL 60515-1426
ivpress.com
email@ivpress.com

InterVarsity Press® is the book-publishing division of InterVarsity Christian Fellowship/USA®, a movement of students and faculty active on campus at hundreds of universities, colleges, and schools of nursing in the United States of America, and a member movement of the International Fellowship of Evangelical Students. For information about local and regional activities, visit intervarsity.org.

All Scripture quotations, unless otherwise indicated, are taken from the New American Standard Bible®, copyright 1960, 1962, 1963, 1968, 1971, 1972, 1973, 1975, 1977, 1995 by The Lockman Foundation. Used by permission.

While any stories in this book are true, some names and identifying information may have been changed to protect the privacy of individuals.

The publisher cannot verify the accuracy or functionality of website URLs used in this book beyond the date of publication.

Cover design and image composite: David Fassett
Interior design: Jeanna Wiggins
Images: clenched fist: © CSA Images / Getty Images
  hand illustration: © CSA Images / Getty Images
  grungy white paper: © enjoynz / iStock / Getty Images
  black ink rolled background: © IntergalacticDesignStudio / E+ / Getty Images
  cardstock texture: © Zakharova_Natalia / iStock / Getty Images

ISBN 978-1-5140-0184-4 (print)
ISBN 978-1-5140-0185-1 (digital)

Printed in the United States of America ∞

InterVarsity Press is committed to ecological stewardship and to the conservation of natural resources in all our operations. This book was printed using sustainably sourced paper.

Library of Congress Cataloging-in-Publication Data

Names: Yancey, George A., 1962- author.
Title: Beyond racial division : a unifying alternative to colorblindness and antiracism / by George Yancey.
Description: Downers Grove, IL : InterVarsity Press, 2022. | Includes bibliographical references.
Identifiers: LCCN 2021053189 (print) | LCCN 2021053190 (ebook) | ISBN 9781514001844 (print) | ISBN 9781514001851 (digital)
Subjects: LCSH: Racism—Religious aspects—Christianity. | Post-racialism.
  | Race relations—Religious aspects—Christianity. | Common good. |
  Racism—United States. | Reconciliation—Religious
  aspects—Christianity.
Classification: LCC BT734.2 .Y36 2022 (print) | LCC BT734.2 (ebook) | DDC 230.08900973—dc23/eng/20211130
LC record available at https://lccn.loc.gov/2021053189
LC ebook record available at https://lccn.loc.gov/2021053190

P 25 24 23 22 21 20 19 18 17 16 15 14 13 12 11 10 9 8 7 6 5 4 3 2 1

Y 41 40 39 38 37 36 35 34 33 32 31 30 29 28 27 26 25 24 23 22

CONTENTS

INTRODUCTION

IMAGINE THAT YOU ARE ON A JOURNEY. You are headed toward a specific destination. Suddenly you come to a fork in the road. You see two clear paths ahead of you, but both make you uncomfortable. You consider the first path. As you look down it, you cannot tell whether it reaches your destination. You ask questions of some who have walked this path before. They say it just circles around back to the start. Oh, it is a pleasant enough path, easily trod. But no matter how long people walk on it, they get no closer to their objective. While this path may be a nice comfortable walk, it will not help you reach your goal.

You look at the other path. It seems to head toward your destination but appears dark and foreboding. Fewer people have returned from this path. Those who have come back warn of dangerous animals ready to pounce. Even though it seems to offer a way to where you want to go, it is a conflict-filled path. You watch as more individuals weaponize to protect themselves. No one comes back to tell you they made it to the end. You do not have any good choices.

Either you select the path leading nowhere or the path full of wild animals.

But then you see a third path! You did not notice this one before. You can see your destination, but brush and fallen debris block the way. There are no signs of wild animals, which brings you relief, but this path is a difficult one. Few if any have traveled this way before. You could ignore this path and choose one of the others, but if you do, it will be harder to get back to this promising third path.

This book offers a way to travel the third path. The path that goes nowhere represents racial colorblindness, which ignores the damage our racialized society has sustained. It seems an easy path, but ultimately it sends us around in circles. The path full of dangerous animals represents antiracism. Evidence suggests that antiracism creates more racial hostility and polarizes us more than it brings us together. The third path is the mutual accountability approach. It promises to be hard. Since not many people have traveled this path, we cannot know all the problems that await us. But we know the other two paths do not work. So why not take this new path?

This illustration reveals the options before us. In these pages I will point out evidence and highlight arguments that support mutual accountability. There is a lot of work involved in implementing this approach, but research indicates it is a superior way to solve our racial problems. This path becomes more difficult to find the longer we stay on the pathways of colorblindness and antiracism. Those efforts have failed, and the longer we pursue them, the harder it is to transition to something with more potential. By the time you reach the end of this book, I hope you will have decided to join me on this journey and see what it holds for us.

CAN WE HAVE A BETTER SOCIETY?

Many of us are tired of fighting the same racial battles over and over again. We are tired of waiting for the next racial controversy to generate more animosity and hostility. We are tired of running into old ideologies that do not serve us well. We are tired of hearing the same arguments and getting nothing done. Those who endorse colorblindness immediately blame those who want to be proactive in dealing with racial issues. Those with an antiracism mindset blame those who are not as active as they are. Those groups talk past each other. Those who are not comfortable with either approach have not been able to find a different path forward and just watch the ongoing conflict. I am going to describe that third path.

If we can stop talking past each other and instead talk to each other, I believe change is possible. We can let the next racial incident lead to a real conversation that brings us together rather than rips us asunder. Maybe I am wrong. Maybe there is no solution and we are trapped in racial polarization. But I refuse to accept that fatalism, which says this is all there is. Yes, this is all there is if we refuse to move out of the colorblindness-antiracism dichotomy. But we do not have to stay here. We can either keep doing what we are doing, or we can try a novel approach. An approach that has not been utilized nearly enough but one we have good reason to think will be effective. If we can develop a movement based on mutual accountability, then we will finally have a chance to break out of our destructive racial cycle.

WHO IS THIS BOOK FOR?

In the subsequent chapters I will more explicitly point out the failures of our previous efforts, rooted mostly in attempts at either colorblindness or antiracism. But for some individuals I do not need to point out these shortcomings. There is a group that wants to address unfair racial outcomes in our society, and ignoring these outcomes is not attractive to them. But they know the antiracism method does not help construct the type of atmosphere where sustainable change is possible. These are "my people." They are the ones looking for a third path, one that does not ignore the racialization of our society but does not drive individuals away with heavy-handed antiracism approaches either.

Of course, many individuals committed to colorblindness are so dedicated that nothing I say will move them. Let's say this is 15 to 20 percent of this country. There is probably a similar-size group committed to antiracism. If this estimation is correct, then 60 to 70 percent of the country may be open to new ways of thinking. Many realize, as I have come to realize, that these paths are going nowhere and instead intensify our racial conflict. Others may favor one approach over the other but still have doubts about it. Wherever you fall, I encourage you to consider a new way of dealing with racial alienation.

Finally, let me tackle a potential barrier for some readers. This book is written by a Christian and published by a Christian publishing house. It is tempting to say the issues brought forward here apply only to Christians. I disagree. Throughout this book I will rely on my personal ideas and empirical research to argue that a mutual accountability model is superior to both colorblindness and antiracism. It is true that my Christian theological beliefs inspired my original considerations of the mutual accountability model, yet my confidence grew as I looked at real-world evidence. It is also true that several of my examples involve Christians and Christian settings. I use chapter six to outline my theological arguments, and that chapter can be valuable for motivating believers to adopt mutual accountability to address racial issues. But if Christianity is not your thing, skip that chapter. In the remaining chapters, I write for a wider audience to give these ideas a fair hearing.

WE NEED A NEW PATH

WHO AM I, and why should you even listen to me? I am a black man. When you are a black man in the United States, it is difficult to escape your racial status. So it should not be surprising that soon after receiving my doctorate in sociology I started conducting research on issues of race and ethnicity. About fifteen years ago I believed I had reached the pinnacle of my career as a race scholar with the publication of two important books (Emerson & Yancey, 2010; Yancey, 2006). Well, at least *I* thought they were important. Not a lot of other people did. I knew the ideas in those books did not conform to traditional ways of thinking about race for either conservatives or progressives. Although the books have generated enough interest to keep them in circulation, they have had a limited audience. Since I felt I had said all I had to say on racial issues, I went on to write and talk about other matters, deciding I would never again do serious writing on racial issues.

Well, "never" does not last as long as one might think. Here I am doing serious writing on race again. Why? What brought me back? On February 23, 2020, Ahmaud Arbery was gunned down while on a run. We had seen shootings of black men before, but this one bothered me more than most. Selfishly, maybe, because I work out by cycling and could see myself in a position like that of Arbery. That is less true in other cases, such as the events involving Michael Brown, Freddie Gray, and Trayvon Martin. But Arbery's killing alone was not enough to drag me back into the fray. It also took the murder of George Floyd on May 25. Perhaps it was being under Covid-19 lockdown. Perhaps it was having two such killings so close together that resonated with me. I cannot say for certain what it was, but it made me tired. I checked out of social media and the news for about three weeks.

When I came back to paying attention and opened myself up to others, I was astounded. All of the sudden I was being contacted by groups wanting to talk to me or have me talk to their group. There was a dramatic increase in radio interview and podcast requests. My books, which were more than a decade old, started to see a resurgence in sales. There was increased interest in my social media accounts.

What created this new interest? I believe it happened because the path I enunciated does not drag individuals toward the mistakes of either colorblindness or antiracism. It confirmed to me that there is an audience of individuals who see the failures of both colorblindness and antiracism. They demand something new. Something they believe can work.

This attention has excited me and confirmed to me that the path I described some years ago is the one we need to take. With the additional experience I have gained since my last work on racial issues, I am ready to dive into this subject again.

I will argue that what I call mutual accountability is the best way to produce a better outcome in our ongoing racial conflict. Before 2020, I could make the excuse that nobody was paying attention. But given the renewed attention I described above, I can no longer make that claim. It is one thing to stay on the sidelines when there is little chance your activism will do any good. It is another matter altogether when you have an opportunity to make a difference. I want to make a difference.

THE PROBLEM IS IN ME

I am going to offer a solution to the racial problems before us. But no matter how good my approach, I must also recognize that I am part of the problem. I live in a racialized society, and I cannot escape the effect of that society. I, the African American race scholar, have a problem with racism.

This reality slapped me in the face when I was in graduate school. During my last year in Austin, Texas, I lived in an interracial neighborhood in the northeastern part of the city. One day while watching the news I heard of a police shooting. The broadcast included the name of the street where the shooting took place, and I realized that it was in my own neighborhood. A man had been harassing a woman and the police drove him off. When the man returned, he produced what they thought was a gun and the police opened fire, killing the man. Was my first thought about the welfare of the man shot? Was it about the woman who may have watched the man die? Was it even about my own security living in a neighborhood where a crime like that could take place? No. My first thought was, "I hope he was not black."

I hope he was not black! Of all the first thoughts to have, why did I focus on race? Because I knew that if this man was black, I would wonder if his race led to his being shot, I would be reminded about the precarious relationships between black men and the police, and I would fear possible new tensions rising in my city and neighborhood. Not only does the skinhead or black nationalist have a problem with racial ethnocentrism, but I do as well. My society has instilled that ethnocentrism within me, and I learned those lessons well. I contribute to the racial alienation plaguing our society and unless I take deliberate steps to do otherwise, I will always be more a part of the problem than the solution.

A major issue inhibiting us from confronting larger institutional and structural racial issues is our own racialized desires, insecurities, and fears. We all occupy a place in this racial structure and we either defend our current position or work to improve that position. What I was not thinking of, and what we tend to not think about, is what is best for everyone. How can I break out of my racialized bubble to put forth answers that reflect more than the reality that I am a black man? How can any of us truly free ourselves from the racialized glue sticking us to our own self-defenses and desires for "our people" to be free to care for all in our society? Recognizing our own weaknesses and biases is a vital first step in dealing with the racial conundrum facing us.

OUR UNHEALTHY CYCLE

As many have said, insanity is doing the same thing over and over again and expecting different results. But we do not have to be insane. We can consider why we have our current racial situation and choose a different route. Have you noticed our unhealthy cycle of racial controversy in the United States? It goes like this: We have a racial incident, such as a police shooting of an African American, and then we have a series of protests demanding justice. After a while there are counterprotests and pushback from those who consider the demands of the protesters to be unreasonable. Finally we return to some kind of normalcy and wait for the next racial incident to start the cycle all over again.

This cycle is the direct result of the fact that we have two contradictory forces fighting for ascendency in our debate on how to deal with racial alienation. After a racial incident, those promoting some version of antiracism become active. For the moment they have the upper hand in the news cycle with their protests and other forms of activism. But over time those supporting a more colorblind approach push back. They argue that antiracists have overplayed their concerns or that this incident is not a real example of racism. The argument shifts, allowing them the opportunity to push their agenda forward. With both groups going at each other, we then return to our stalemate between the forces of colorblindness and antiracism.

Generally speaking, strong adherents in either group do not alter their perspective due to the new racial incident. Instead they become more entrenched in the rightness of their cause. But soon the attention of the public is drawn to a different event or situation and the momentum to deal with our racialized society begins to evaporate. Neither those advocating colorblindness nor those supporting antiracism have been reduced in numbers or social power, so they remain ready to fight on a new day. Any political or social victories won by either side of this racialized debate are short-lived due to the reality that another powerful social group stands ready to resist those victories. The fight, and the cycle, go on.

As long as we are convinced that these are our only two options, this process will continue for the foreseeable future. One possible outcome is that eventually either colorblindness or antiracism will win out and that side will implement long-term social and political reforms according to their own desires. That is a possibility, and I am certain both groups would like to see it occur for their own cause. But it is not likely to happen soon, and in the meantime more social damage will be done in our racial wars. Furthermore, do we think the vanquished group will just go away? Or will they stick around and do all they can to ruin the reforms promoted by the victors?

We can pick a side to fight for and wait to see which group will win, or we can acknowledge that these racial wars are not good for our society and figure out how to work together. We badly need to find solutions that are not short-term but sustainable in a racialized society, since multiple groups have "skin" in the game. This is the only way for us, in any reasonable time frame, to reduce or even eliminate our sick cycle of racial event, protest, counterprotest, normalcy, and new racial event that continues to plague us.

MODELS FOR CONFRONTING RACIAL ISSUES

When I discussed racial issues in my original book (2006) I talked about four different models by which we try to deal with racial issues. Those models were colorblindness, Anglo-conformity, multiculturalism, and white responsibility. Much of what I described in the white responsibility model can now be considered antiracism. Many of the tenets of multiculturalism have recently been co-opted by advocates of antiracism as well. But they focus less on honoring all cultures, which is theoretically the goal of multiculturalism, and rather demand adherence to the values and ideals found in antiracism. This leads not to a spirit of multiculturalism but an assertion that we need the right culture to eliminate racism.

Much of what I ascribed to Anglo-conformity is less popular today. Anglo-conformity focused on teaching people of color to move toward economic success with an emphasis on an acceptance of Western European values and methods. But just as multicultural efforts have largely been replaced with antiracism, so too have Anglo-conformity efforts been replaced with a greater emphasis on colorblindness. While it has not completely disappeared, I do not see the push for solutions based in Anglo-conformity that was prevalent a couple of decades ago. Thus it makes more sense to talk about colorblindness as the dominant ideology rather than Anglo-conformity.

In summary, when it comes to dealing with racial problems, it is clear that today we are looking at two competing dominant ideologies rather than four. These two ideologies have the social and cultural resources to be available to the larger population. But there is a better way.

MUTUAL ACCOUNTABILITY

In previous works I have also spoken of mutual obligation or mutual responsibility when it comes to issues of race. Today I prefer the phrase *mutual accountability*. But if this is not clear, the main element of this model can be described with another two-word concept: collaborative conversations. A collaborative conversation has been defined (Brake, 2019) as "a purposeful, outcome-driven conversation aimed at building on each other's ideas." The key to this process is that everyone is allowed to participate, and everyone's ideas are taken seriously. Everyone has a say in the final outcome. A willingness to participate in the conversation and to make room for the contributions of others is expected. We are all accountable to find solutions that best serve everybody, thus the term *mutual accountability*. For the balance of the book I will use *mutual accountability* and *collaborative conversations* interchangeably.

Mutual accountability is not an insistence that we find equal and identical roles for everyone in our society. It is about our mutual responsibility to enter into the conversation. The outcome will be worked out in that conversation. To use an analogy, if a husband is going out with his male friends too much, he and his wife have a responsibility to discuss a solution they can live with. It is not for her to dictate how much and how often he can go out with them. She may not want him to go out at all, but he has a need for their companionship. It is not up to the husband to decide either. He must take his wife's needs into account. Rather, they both enter a collaborative conversation to find the best solution for their relationship.

Notice what has not happened. The wife has not been asked to cut down on time spent on her relationships with her female friends, because that was not the problem at hand. If the husband has not been troubled by her time with friends, then it is merely vindictive to insist that she curtail those relationships. The husband and wife have a mutual responsibility to enter into a healthy conversation, but the solution does not require that both parties play an equal role.

In the larger racial context, it is possible that the outcome of our collaborative conversations will involve minimizing the different racial dynamics of each group with the solution grounded in a colorblind mentality. Since it is important not to preordain solutions, I concede that a race-neutral solution is possible. But I seriously doubt this will happen. Given the racial ugliness in our country and the way people of color have suffered, it is unlikely they will settle for a solution that ignores the effects of historical racism and institutional bias. I think the most likely outcome is one where the roles of the races are different, although we share in the responsibility to enter into the dialogue in a respectful manner.

The path of mutual accountability is capable of leading us out of our current cycle because its focus is not purely on winning the argument. This is not to say we ignore our own concerns. Rather, we find a venue where we can air our concerns and have them heard. In return we listen to the concerns of others. In that atmosphere of collaborative communication, we work together to find solutions we can accept. We break the cycle because we learn we cannot have everything. We cannot expect to gain domination over our political or racial opponents. But we find ways of working together. When we do that, the cycle of protest and counter-protest can be replaced by a process of communication, mutual solutions, and then labor from all sides to make the solutions successful.

Why would those steeped in our previous models of color-blindness and antiracism consider communication and compromise when they are so convinced they are in the right? Some individuals will be resistant. But they need to consider that their chances of getting everything they want are slim. Their political victories will continue to be sabotaged by their opponents. What if they could get most of what they want with their political opponents helping instead of hindering them? If we bring people into discussion and find compromises, then we gain real allies instead of inspiring opposition. The mutual accountability approach is our best effort to find stable, sustainable solutions that pull us together rather than tear us apart.

TALKING TO EACH OTHER

Since communication is important in this approach, it is essential to define certain terms. I do so with the goal of having the terms be accessible to everyone. The way we communicate can either shut people out of the conversation or bring them into the conversation. Research indicates that when individuals are approached in ways that feel threatening, they stop considering arguments from the source of the threat (Chapman, 2012; May, 2007; McNamee, 2011). It does no good to complain about their unwillingness to have those conversations. As human beings we have certain psycho-logical defenses that kick into action when we hear threat-ening arguments. The way we talk to each other matters. It does not matter if we're right if we cannot communicate our perspective to those who disagree.

For example, I have often heard whites talk about how they "do not see color." I have talked to enough whites to under-stand the sentiment behind such assertions. The person is letting me know he or she will not treat me in a negative way because of my race. Because I understand this, I am not of-fended. However, I know how tone-deaf this statement comes across to many people of color. To say our race does not matter flies in the face of our life experience. Being black is an important part of who I am. To say you do not see that is to say you do not see an important aspect of my identity. Worse, if you ask me to ignore my race, you are asking me to ignore a part of myself. You are saying I cannot bring my entire self into relationship with you.

Now, I believe many people of color understand that race has not been an important aspect of most white people's lives, so white people struggle to see the importance of race. And not recognizing the impact of race on oneself is different from a blanket assertion that race does not, or should not, matter. It leaves open the possibility of learning about how one's racial identity impacts nonwhites. I know that many whites who seem like they are dismissing the role of race in society actually have good intentions and do not intend to dismiss me. But some people of color feel threatened by this idea and are unable to listen further to what these individuals have to say.

People of color can also frame important ideas in ways that make those ideas inaccessible to people outside their ideological circles. This often centers around the way a term such as *racism* is used. You probably will not see that word in this book as much as you might expect. It is not because I am unaware of its permutations or how to apply it in an academically useful manner. Rather, *racism* is a term that, used the wrong way, can shut down productive conversations. Many people connect the word *racism* to white hoods and skinheads and therefore check out of the conversation when it comes up. To that end, I will forego talking about a "racist" or "white supremacist" society. My experience is that those who do not already accept the concept of the United States being a racist or white supremacist society will unlikely be moved by further claims that it is such a society. They are likely to feel they are being blamed for all of society's problems and close their minds to further discussion.

I prefer to talk about the United States as a "racialized" society. Our racial identity impacts our standing in this society. It is not the only thing that matters. It is often not even the most important thing that matters. But who can argue that race does not matter at all? There is much research showing that it matters quite negatively for people of color. In chapter three we will look at some of that research. But for now, I will refer to the United States as a "racialized" rather than "racist" society. This lets me discuss the negative impact of racialization in a way that allows more people to hear my concerns.

RACIAL ALIENATION

In the mutual accountability model, we have to work together to find acceptable solutions to our racial problems. But our racial alienation is a major barrier preventing us from identifying and implementing those solutions. While the natural response of a race scholar might be to focus on racism, once again that term comes with all sorts of baggage. Also, talking about the problems of racism produces a tendency to think those problems are due only to the actions of whites. The approach I advocate places responsibility on everyone.

Even in a society where whites have dominant power and often maintain systems that reinforce that power, people of color do not lack agency. Indeed, we have more agency than at any other time of our history, and the way we use that agency will help shape the nature of race relations. I do not see the utility of using "racism" to discuss the problems we face, because even though racism exists, it is a mistake to imply that all our racial issues stem directly from it. Even as racism continues to rear its ugly head, racial alienation prevents us from finding sustainable solutions to our racial problems.

By "racial alienation," I mean that our ability to connect with each other and work out our problems together has been badly damaged. We are separated from each other and relate to each other in unhealthy ways. This separation is not merely physical, although it is that, but it is also in relationships and in purpose. This separation affects our thinking, as we tend to focus on perspectives and ideas that further the interests of our own racial, and sometimes political, group. Separation is the natural consequence of centuries of racial abuse. Continued alienation feeds our ongoing racial conflict and makes it difficult for us to function in a healthy way in an interracial society. Our challenge is to overcome the effects of those centuries of abuse and rebuild a racialized society where this type of separation is reduced and perhaps even eliminated.

The concept of racial alienation does not mean we bear equal responsibility in the creation of the conditions that led to this alienation. Historical racism has created our racial hierarchy, and the social structures that come out of that racism continue to affect people of color negatively. But how do we move beyond these effects to find lasting racial solutions for our society? In the past many of those solutions have come about through activism and protest. But I am skeptical of the efficacy of that route today.

THE MODERN CIVIL RIGHTS MOVEMENT

Protest and political activism are natural responses to racial abuse. Racial discrimination was particularly severe in the middle of the twentieth century, so it's not surprising that in the 1950s and 1960s we saw an increase in protest generated by civil rights movements in response to the plight of racial minorities. In a society where the humanity of nonwhites was constantly questioned, once nonwhites gained a voice to express their fate, it was to be expected that they would use that voice to fight for a sense of humanity.

Some individuals think the civil rights movement started with Martin Luther King Jr. It didn't. Indeed, the black church has been a driving force of racism resistance since the early days of slavery. Triumphs by individuals such as W. E. B. Du Bois and Thurgood Marshall predated King's successes. However, there is a reason people believe King launched the modern civil rights movement. King saw great value in creating a racially integrated civil rights movement. Unlike individuals such as Malcolm X, who had a separatist perspective that made it difficult for him to work with whites, King sought alliances with whites. In helping them redeem their "souls" after their connections to a racist society, he hoped to work with them to bring about racial equality. King did not shy away from calling out the racism of his day. He was not hesitant to go after individual whites, such as Bull Connor, who engaged in racism. But he did not go after whites as a race.

In 1965 the Student Nonviolent Coordinating Committee (SNCC) developed and, within it, the black power movement was launched. Two other black nationalist groups, the Black Panthers and Black Muslims (forerunners to the Nation of Islam), also supported more revolutionary visions of the United States. The actions of these activists signaled a desire to overturn a racist society. Who could blame them? After generations of racial abuse, would it not be appropriate for the abuse to end immediately? Even King in his famous "Letter from Birmingham Jail" lays out why blacks should not keep waiting for whites to grant them what they should have by common humanity—their basic civil rights. If whites were reluctant to give people of color what was due them, why not take it by force? Why not take it by revolution?

But Americans were not ready for revolution. The civil rights movement lost much steam in the latter twentieth century. Protests continued, but with the passing of the Civil Rights Act of 1964 and Voting Rights Act of 1965, dealing with racial issues did not retain the same sense of urgency. Furthermore, a powerful backlash developed that served to blunt further efforts of the movement. What some have called the "second reconstruction" inevitably led to a decline in the influence and power of the modern civil rights movement (Bartley & Graham, 2019; Marable, 1984), and the emerging Reagan Revolution further weakened its impact (Bonilla-Silva, 2020; Zuckerman, 2011). A change of public opinion occurred during the Reagan years, with fewer individuals per-ceiving the civil rights movement as successful (Santoro, 2015).

This did not mean the end of racial protests against racial inequality. But our society began to experience the cycle of racial event, protest, counterprotest, normalcy, equilibrium, and new racial event. The periods of unrest did not last long enough to lead to the type of political and legal break-throughs that came about during King's time. Resistance to the more aggressive approach that emerged after King's career has also limited the continuing success of the modern civil rights movement. Thus the movement has not seen the same level of success it did with the adoption of important legislation in its early years.

Perhaps we do not see such legislation because the nature of racism has so dramatically changed. Overtly racist laws have largely been eradicated. Newer problems lie in subtle racial prejudice and the lingering effects of historical racism. It is difficult to conceive of laws that would be effective against this type of racial disadvantage. Also, it is not always clear what protesters want. It is easy to say "Black lives matter" but much harder to conceptualize how to put that into law. One can complain about white privilege, but how do you construct laws that end it? Protests during the early years of the modern civil rights movement had explicit goals and aims in mind. There were specific laws inhibiting the rights of blacks to vote, to live where they wanted to live, and to work at jobs for which they had the proper qualifications. Overturning those laws was a concrete focus, which aided the protests. In the protests today, demands are often wide reaching, and they sometimes read like an ever-growing wish list rather than demands for specific rights.

Arguably the greatest achievement of the modern civil rights movement was not the passage of any given law, as important as those laws were, but the recentering of racial attitudes away from accepting white supremacy and toward demanding racial tolerance. The emergence of a multiracial movement likely led to more personal interracial relationships and more productive communication between members of racial groups. It was not just political power and activism but also the building of relationships across the racial spectrum that was important. While past activism is important, it is in the past. We face different challenges and opportunities today.

THE BIG QUESTION

When I was in graduate school, I fell in love for the first time. She was attractive and I was on cloud nine that she wanted me. But her mother did not want me. More specifically, her mother, who happened to be a well-educated professional and self-described "feminist," did not want her white daughter to date a black man. I believed that if I could meet my girlfriend's mother, I could show her what a good man I was and change her mind. But she refused even to meet me. She eventually forced her daughter to break up with me. It broke my heart.

Heartbreak is probably normal in the loss of all first loves, but it was particularly painful that I lost the relationship purely because of racism. It was a turning point in my life. Up until that point I had known racism existed and experienced it myself. But I'd believed I could overcome any barriers racism placed before me. I naively felt that once people got to know me, they would not hold on to their racist stereotypes and would treat me fairly. My experience with my girlfriend showed me that racism was so pervasive and powerful that there were barriers I could not overcome no matter how competent, likable, or moral I was. Because of this ugly racism, a woman who would not even meet with me judged me for being black. If this racism had not personally impacted me, I am not certain I would have developed the level of interest I have today in confronting this cancer.

A few years ago an old friend called me to catch up. She confided to me a problem her high school son was having. My friend's son, who is white, was being romantically pursued by a black girl. He happened not to like her, although it had nothing to do with her being black. She was just not his type. Yet he feared it would get around the school that he was racist for refusing to go out with her. The overt racism that was so freely practiced when I was in graduate school was now stigmatized. I have lived long enough to see a society go from one where a woman can openly express her racism by pressuring her daughter to reject a black man simply because he is black to one where the mere appearance of not wanting to date interracially can result in being labeled a racist.

We have not eliminated racism from our society. But we have made it a great deal more taboo. Given my experience in dealing with overt racism, I am happy to see it stigmatized. This means we no longer argue about my worth as a person of color. If my situation occurred today, I do not believe a professional feminist woman would refuse to meet her daughter's black boyfriend. Can you imagine the hostility she would face? If she had any type of job that dealt with the public, she could lose that job. I suspect that some of her friends would shun her as well if news of her overt racism got out. Even if she was secretly racist, she would have to find a pretense of refusing to support the relationship rather than relying on an obvious racist justification. It is good that my sons are unlikely to face the situation I faced with someone who refuses to meet them simply because of their race. My comfort that they will never face such a situation reflects the revolution of our racial values even within my lifetime.

It is important to recognize the significant changes our society has experienced. Failure to do so causes us to employ arguments that are no longer in play. We are not arguing today about whether people of color are fully human. Those who believe otherwise are few and far between. Yes, they can do violence and damage, but they do not hold significant public opinion. If we focus on that argument, we will use up resources trying to answer a question that is not on the table. We are not debating whether overt racism is socially acceptable.[1] The vast majority of Americans take it as a given that people of color should have the same rights as others.

Rather, the major debate today is about how we compensate for the centuries of racial abuse that plagued our nation historically. It focuses on how we envision a fair society considering the historical injustices people of color have faced. So the big question we must struggle with is this: *How do we recover from our history of racial abuse in ways most of us consider to be fair?* This is the central question that all attempts to end racism must address. It takes into consideration how historical racism has influenced our current economic and cultural hierarchy as well as how racial prejudice manifests in a contemporary context. Determining the direction we need to go in contemporary American society continues to fuel our racial debate.

CREATING FAIRNESS IN CONTEMPORARY SOCIETY

When you observe those pushing for racial activism and those resisting such activism, you can see the big question playing out in our larger society. People answer the question of how we create a fair society after centuries of racial abuse differently, which generates continuing conflict.

People of color have approached that question with a powerful desire to create a society they see as fair. Generally they are less positive about fairness in the United States (Jost, Whitfield, & Jost, 2005; O'Brien & Major, 2005; Peffley & Hurwitz, 2010), so they want to see changes to make society fair. The need for such change was clear during the beginning of the modern civil rights movement when the very humanity of African Americans was in question. Despite the advances that have been made, many people of color feel the same way today. They recognize we do not have the same types of oppression that we did in the past, but oppression manifests itself in different ways. They argue that we still live in a society dominated by white supremacy even though there is little appetite for overt white supremacy today. This creates a desire among people of color to continue with protests and activism until they obtain what they perceive as fair. If you believe that society is still not fair for people of color, it makes sense that you want to see greater public and private efforts to create that fair society.

Of course, this is not how many whites see the situation. They believe our society is already fair. In their eyes any reforms beyond the civil rights legislation we currently have will accrue unfair advantages to people of color. They see today's activism as a way for racial minorities to turn a fair society into an unfair one. They may look approvingly on the activism of the 1960s, believing it was necessary to rid society of overt racism. But because most whites do not take seriously the issues of historical racism and institutional discrimination, they do not see the need for a contemporary civil rights movement. Their assumption is that since we have overcome overt racism, any efforts to make things "fairer" will be inequitable for whites. They believe that when resources are targeted for people of color, those resources are taken away from whites, especially poor whites. Acceptance of a colorblind notion that we should avoid providing special aid for people of color makes sense in light of those assumptions.

Again, our dysfunctional racial cycle is driven by the conflict of determining what is fair in our racialized society. The two visions put before us are not reconcilable without the give-and-take of healthy communication. But that communication is all but impossible since individuals on both sides of the racial divide are convinced they are correct and see no need to compromise. They see such compromise as producing an unfair society because it detracts from their own vision of racial fairness. Until we find pathways to healthy communication, these differing views of fairness will continue to feed the unhealthy racialization of our society.

CONCLUSION

There are those wedded to philosophies that served them well in the past but do not do so today. A purely colorblind approach that completely ignores race was a very progressive racial position for much of our country's history. However, the racial abuse that accumulated over the centuries makes such an attitude untenable for many people of color. The failure of many whites to recognize the historical and contemporary ways race still matters in our society by latching onto a philosophy that does not represent the realities of people of color inhibits our attempts to lessen racial alienation. While many complaints about antiracism are legitimate, at least attempts at antiracism are addressing real social problems. One cannot respond to a solution, even a flawed solution, with nothing but inactivity.

On the other hand, sometimes generals fight old battles in current wars. They assume tactics that were successful in the past will also be successful in present battles. But old strategies lose their effectiveness. Past activism took place in a time when the goals were clearer and the question was about the basic humanity of racial minorities. That activism was carried out in a way that forced whites to confront that humanity. It led to a longtime alteration in attitudes, which helped stabilize the legal and political changes emerging from those activists' efforts.

Today, however, we see many examples of activism failing to accomplish the desired goals. Take, for instance, recent events in Southlake, Texas (Hixenbaugh, 2021). In 2018, a video went public showing white high school students uttering the N-word and laughing. As you might imagine, there was an uproar. Parents of color and activists went to school board meetings and let their concerns be heard. The school board eventually developed a plan for diversity and inclusion training in their K–12 curriculum. But the board's actions spurred a backlash from many white parents in the district, who made arguments about "diversity police" and reverse racism. A lawsuit put the plan on hold. The battle caught the attention of state Republican politicians, who castigated the activists' efforts in order to score political points. Unless something drastically changes, the diversity plan is not likely to see the light of day.[2] The cycle has struck again. Activism that might have produced lasting results during the civil rights movement usually creates a backlash today that threatens the sustainability of reforms emerging from that activism.

When we come to such an impasse, the answer is not to dig in deeper and refuse to recognize the value of other perspectives. Political wins we enjoy today can become political defeats we feel tomorrow. A better answer is to find ways to communicate with each other. We are all accountable for creating the type of atmosphere where productive racial dialogue is possible.

THE MUTUAL
ACCOUNTABILITY
MODEL

I SAT ACROSS FROM LEROY, a middle-aged African American man. We were having lunch not long after the election of President Donald Trump. The discouragement on his face was evident. He talked to me of his disappointment in the election results and the fact that so many of his white friends had voted for Trump.[1]

This was more than political disagreement. Yes, Leroy had been a Democrat his entire life. For him they were the party that cared about him and his community. He did not agree with everything in the Democratic platform, but he appreciated their attention to issues of social justice. Still, over the years he had also come to understand why many of his white friends voted for Republicans, as they saw them as the party of life and family values. But Trump? No way could they support a man who had demonstrated such a high level of immorality and blatant disregard for people of color. Until they did.

I had few words to comfort my friend. I shared his frustration. We both acknowledged that the 2016 vote felt like a stab in the back for us as African Americans. It was like our white brothers and sisters did not even want to listen to us. Before the election Leroy and I had shared with many of our white friends our concerns about having a president who trafficked in race-baiting and appealed to the worst elements of the Republican party—elements we had personally experienced as effects of historical and contemporary racism. For us this was not merely a political disagreement. This was about whether race relations were going to be set back severely.

After the election, we both were at a crossroads. Did we pull away from those we felt had betrayed us? Or did we lean in and try to repair the damage done? I cannot tell you what Leroy did, because he is a compilation of many people of color I communicated with after Trump's election. Some pulled back. Some leaned in. But it was not merely the election that created this reaction. This mistrust has built over time through a history of racial abuse. It is a mistrust reinforced by the actions, intentional and otherwise, of whites indicating a disregard for our racial struggles. Events like the election of Donald Trump were the final straw for some people of color, who washed their hands of dealing with or trying to understand the perspective of whites. While I understand that sentiment, I find no hope going down that route. So I must lean in.

How do we get past this barrier of mistrust? How do we find a solution that serves everyone and not just our chosen group? We need a path forward that compensates for our tendency to focus on the needs of our group and ignore those of others. We must change how we communicate with each other, because what we are doing now is not working. We need an approach that not only meets the needs of most individuals but has a chance of gaining support across racial and political lines. It is with those ideas in mind that I discuss the mutual accountability approach.

THE ESSENCE OF MUTUAL ACCOUNTABILITY

So how do we find solutions that go beyond the needs of our own group? Let us dispense with one seemingly easy solution. We may be tempted to say that *our* chosen approach will create the best solutions for everyone, not just those in our group. That sounds great in theory, but it underestimates the power of confirmation and self-interest bias. We humans have a natural ability to convince ourselves that what we ourselves want is best for everyone concerned. In doing this we can be blind to the needs of others. We should have little confidence that our own solutions are free from a self-serving bias and truly meet the needs of everybody.

Ever been in the middle of a church split? I have. It was not pleasant. It was the classic example of a church with older individuals who were entrenched in the status quo and a younger cohort who wanted changes. Both groups felt they were doing what was best for the entire church. Neither group (including, I admit, the younger cohort, of which I was a part) seriously considered the interests of the other. For example, the older cohort was resistant to all changes in the musical style. They felt their traditional music was

honoring to God and best for the church. It was connected
to tradition and values essential to the founding of the
church. Those in the younger cohort felt the music had to
change with the times and help make the church relevant.
Looking back now I can see that both groups had legitimate
concerns. But we could not work our differences out because members of both groups clearly believed their position was best, and neither of us fully considered the needs
of the other group. Even if you have not been part of a
church split, I bet you have seen this dynamic play itself out
in some other organization.

Often in our confidence that we have found the best path
we presume to speak for everyone involved. We convince ourselves, just like the two factions in my church split, that what
we are doing is for the greater good. We truly believe we are
doing right by others. But what we are generally doing, even
if we do not realize it at the time, is spinning what we want as
the best thing for everyone else. We ignore evidence that what
we want may harm others and amplify evidence that it will
help them. That is the way confirmation bias works.

If we cannot on our own simply consider the interests of
others, what are we to do? This is where the accountability
element is critical. If I want to find solutions that serve the
interests of everyone, I must listen to everyone. I consider
their interests and perspectives and allow them to articulate
those interests and perspectives in their own words. Instead
of coming to my own conclusions and rationalizing why my
solutions are best for everyone, I am obligated to gain the
input of others so that their concerns are heard and

incorporated into any path we take in our efforts to deal with racial alienation.

I will never know if that church could have been saved. But what if instead of venting our frustration at the other side during our meetings we actually tried to talk to each other? What if both sides worked together to solve the problems before us in ways that met the needs of all? What if we sought win-win solutions rather than win-lose solutions? Concerning music, we could have held separate worship services devoted to traditional music and contemporary music, as I saw other churches do later in my life. Such an obvious solution, yet we never tried to implement it. To be sure there were other conflicts that were not so easy to solve, and I do not want to make this too simplistic. But we did not listen to each other enough to even try to solve our problems. Instead we went to war. Kind of like the racial war we are in today.

We would have avoided a lot of pain with a mutual accountability approach. What is the essence of the mutual accountability model? This model stipulates that we work to have healthy interracial communications so that we can solve racial problems. In those communications we strive to listen to those in other racial groups and attempt to account for their interests. In this way we fashion solutions to racialized problems that address the needs of individuals across racial groups instead of promoting solutions that are accepted only by certain racial groups. By allowing those we disagree with to hold us "accountable" to their interests, we are forced to confront the ways we have fashioned solutions that conform to our own interests and desires.

Let me clarify what I mean by "mutual." By this I mean we all, regardless of race and political outlook, have a responsibility to engage in interracial communication in a healthy manner. This means a constructive approach where we listen to others and find relevant ways to communicate with them. Efforts to cut off voices, whether by whites or nonwhites, are not allowed. What mutual does *not* mean is that we find solutions where the ultimate responsibilities of individuals in racial groups and the costs members of these groups pay are identical. Given our history of racial abuse, it seems to me unlikely that we will ultimately come to solutions involving identical responsibilities for members of different racial groups. But to get to solutions that work, we must enter into healthy conversations where everyone is responsible for communicating collaboratively rather than dehumanizing those in other racial groups.

POWER OR MORAL SUASION

What if your child is unwilling to clean up his room? How do you get him to start doing so? Or say your friend is dating a guy who is emotionally manipulative and even abusive. You fear for her safety. How do you get through to her? Or you are teaching a student who needs to put more time into his studies. Can you get him to do that? Or your aunt is picking up toxic QAnon philosophy. How do you show her the error of those ideas? Of course, one option is not to try to convince your son, friend, student, or aunt to change at all. But we often are in situations where, despite our desire to allow people to do what they want, we feel it is important to intervene. We think it necessary to help someone minimize the pain they or others will suffer and help them go down a different path. When we feel the need to intervene, how do we convince others to go down that other path?

If we want to persuade someone to change, we have the options of using power, moral suasion, or reason. And, to be honest, reason is overrated. Most of us are not driven by reason as much as we like to think we are. Social dynamics such as confirmation bias and groupthink interfere with our ability to rely on our intellect to make decisions, especially when those decisions are tied to emotional commitments to previous ideas. If reason is not a reliable way to produce attitudinal change, we are left with power and moral suasion. We can change someone's ways by using social, political, legal, or some other form of power, or we can find a way to persuade them that making that change is the right thing to do. With rare exception, when people make changes due to the influence of others, there is some degree of power or moral suasion at play.

Let's look first at power. There are many forms of power that can be used. A parent obviously has some power over a child. Legal power can be used to hand out punishment. Social power can be used to stigmatize anyone who does not submit to certain demands or change their attitudes. Those with material resources can offer to give or withhold those resources. The ways power can be used to motivate action are endless. There are times when power needs to be used. I want the police officer to use power to stop the bank robber. As a parent I need to exercise my power to stop my young boys from making foolish decisions, such as hitting their brother. I have used physical power to stop physical altercations. Power is a necessary tool in certain situations.

But there is a cost to using power. When we use power successfully, it becomes easier to rely on it to get what we want. Then we live by overpowering others to get our way. As an example, the people of Cuba justifiably used power to throw off the oppressive regime of Fulgencio Batista. But then they installed Fidel Castro as leader, who went on to use his newfound power to continue oppressing Cubans. Those who gain through power often are unwilling to relinquish it once they have it. Furthermore, their expressions of power generally serve to divide members of the community into supporters and resisters of that power.

If reason is ineffective in producing change and power carries its own dangers, what we have left is moral suasion. We persuade an individual that it is right to change his or her mind or to take certain actions. Once people become convinced the new action is the moral thing to do, then change is likely to occur. When some people think of moral suasion, they envision a wild-eyed evangelical preaching incessantly or a liberal professor indoctrinating students. Nothing could be further from the truth. Real moral suasion requires that we build rapport with those we want to persuade (Cialdini, 2001). It means we accurately understand their point of view (Watkins, 2001). We also learn to admit when they are correct and become willing to find areas of agreement (Paulus, 2006). In other words, real moral suasion is about relationship building, not browbeating. Moral suasion, done properly, unites us by making us want to identify with and care for each other. It makes us want to work with others to find out what is good for them. Real moral suasion builds community.

The mutual accountability model is about moral suasion. It is about engaging in conversation so we can bring about healthy change. Power unites only through fear of being punished or of not getting rewards from the person in power. Mutual accountability is focused on building community through dialogue and relationships. It focuses on working out our problems rather than forcing others to do what we want. If moral suasion and relationship building become the approach used to construct our racial future, then we can find workable compromises instead of continual conflict. We can have less saber rattling on social media and political talk shows and more discussions where we understand the perspective of others. We can figure out solutions that do not denigrate others and invite those who disagree with us to help create solutions alongside us.

We can see this process at work in other areas of our lives. In our interpersonal relationships we know it is not healthy to overpower each other. We have seen how damaging it is when one spouse consistently dominates the other. We see friendships where one person controls the other and wince at the manipulation playing out before us. We know these marriages and friendships would be qualitatively better if partners and friends learned how to communicate with each other and found solutions that met the needs of both individuals. Humans are not built to thrive when we overpower others. It tends to bring out the worst in us. While there are times when we must use power in a relationship, in the real world we know that good relationships are built using moral suasion instead.

ACTIVE LISTENING AND MUTUAL ACCOUNTABILITY

If we want to see race relations rebuilt through moral suasion rather than power and domination, it is vital that we learn the tools and techniques needed for collaborative conversation. Our greatest challenge is learning to listen. Most of us find it easier to talk about what we want than to listen to what others want. We are eager to tell our spouse what is wrong with him or her, but we do not want to hear what we have done wrong ourselves. But to engage in mutual accountability, we must listen—not merely for information, but to comprehend the perspective of the other person and truly understand why they believe and feel the way they do. There are different terms for this type of listening, but the one I like is *active listening*.

As a social scientist I use active listening whenever I interview research subjects or conduct focus groups. Active listening is listening for understanding, not argument. Too often when we discuss a controversial issue, we listen only so we can make a counterargument against the speaker. There is a time and place for that approach, but to overcome our tribalistic instincts we must temporarily suppress that impulse. Active listening is an important way to build win-win solutions since we are trying not to win an argument but to understand the other person's perspective.

The key to active listening is to put the attitudes and perceptions of the person into our own words in such a way that they agree with what we are saying. For example, several years ago I coauthored a book on atheism (Williamson & Yancey, 2013). In preparing to write that book my partner and I interviewed over fifty atheists, and I personally interviewed about two dozen atheists. I am not an atheist. But when I heard my respondents make a point about why they thought a theological belief was false, I made it a practice to offer my interpretation of their statement and ask them to correct me if I was wrong. I did not want my theistic beliefs to interfere with my ability to understand my atheist respondents, so I tried, imperfectly, to put myself in their shoes. We have to make similar efforts to understand one another if we want to make progress on racial issues.

When we actively listen, we have a responsibility to rephrase what the other person is saying in such a way that they agree we have captured their ideas honestly. Anything less than this and we have not truly listened actively. If I am trying to understand why someone hates the Black Lives Matter movement, I need to listen to them and then rephrase their reasoning so that they say, "Yes, you understand why I cannot stand that group." If we want to know why someone wants to take down Confederate statues, we need to be able to state their purpose in wanting to see the end of those statues in our own words. We must enunciate their desire to tear down those statues in a way that they will say, "Now you get it why I cannot be satisfied if those statues remain up." The power to say you have actively listened to someone else is not in your hands. It is in the hands of the speaker.

When I speak on this topic, I suggest a little exercise. First, I ask my audience to go have lunch, coffee, or a beer with someone they know disagrees with them on a racial issue. Then they talk to them about that issue. They listen and try to put the other person's ideas into their own words. I ask my audience to actively listen to the other person without expecting that they will then turn around and participate in active listening as well (if they do, then all the better). This exercise helps us learn how to actively listen and how to understand the perspectives of those who do not agree with us. If you get nothing else from this book, try this exercise. It will help you become a better active listener, which will not only help you implement a mutual accountability model but also make you a better communicator overall.

Beyond learning about the perspectives of others, what is the value of active listening? Imagine the next racial incident occurring. When you choose to enter into dialogue with a person you disagree with about that incident, you can do so in such a way that they know you understand them. They will feel heard, and we know that people who feel heard are more open to alternative perspectives. Furthermore, when we feel threatened, we turn off our ability to hear different ideas (Kaplan, Gimbel, & Harris, 2016). You will also know what not to say. If you have a more progressive bent, you will know that characterizing your ideological opponents as white supremacists is a sure way to close their ears. If you have a more conservative bent, you know that saying you do not see race will make people of color feel invisible to you. You have a chance to discuss these issues collaboratively and productively rather than instigating more racial confrontation.

I am not perfect in my attempts to actively listen. I do not want anyone to think I have mastered this skill beyond any need to improve. Many times I have left research interviews and realized I did not truly understand a particular answer given to me. I wished I had followed up with better questions and truly gotten to the bottom of their perspective. In my personal life I often do not engage in active listening even when it would make me a better husband, father, and friend. I tire sometimes, or I am distracted and do not want to do the hard work of listening in this way. And do not get me started on my failings in social media. This is a skill that will take a lifetime to master and to practice. Even after my years of experience as an interviewer, it is a skill I still fall short of possessing to the fullest extent. So if you fall short, do not beat yourself up. Get up off the ground and resolve to do better next time.

DOES THE SPEAKER HAVE RESPONSIBILITIES?

I have talked about listening. But it is worth considering whether those who are speaking bear responsibility as well. In other words, when we are relating our concerns to others, are there ways we can be more efficient? It is in our best interest to do as good a job as possible since their reaction can help determine if we will gain a partner in finding racial solutions.

Perhaps the first step to being a better communicator is not to abuse the respect being given you by those who are actively listening. They are making a commitment to give you the benefit of the doubt. This is not the time to be abusive and insulting. Of course, you should express your feelings and perspectives. You should own those feelings and perspectives. Perhaps the person with whom you are communicating has done something that offends you. It is okay to say you have been offended. It is not okay to state that this was the person's intent, because that is not in your area of knowledge. Some degree of venting will occur. Just remember that we do not have to be accusatory in our venting, nor do we have to be belittling. In a situation of mutual accountability, the person to whom you are venting will have an opportunity to vent back to you. Treat them the way you want to be treated when it is your turn to listen.

Next, try to find concepts the other person can relate to. When I talk with different audiences, I emphasize selective facts I know will be relevant to them. If I am speaking to a more progressive audience, I talk about the importance of justice. I emphasize the lack of efficacy of an antiracist approach. When I talk with a white conservative Christian audience, I point out work I have done showing that their Christian kids are more likely to date outside their faith than their race (Yancey, Hubbard, & Smith, 2009) to indicate that they cannot ignore the racism in their own communities. I am not lying in either instance, but I do emphasize points that are most relevant to them. I understand those values because I have put in the work of actively listening to members of each group. Active listening makes us better communicators because we know how to reach people with topics they find important.

Furthermore, I have found that stories or word pictures can often help us connect with others. If we can find illustrations—often illustrations from the experiences and lives of those with whom we are talking—we have a better chance of conveying our thoughts and even emotions. When I talk to my students, I sometimes tell them about what it is like to be the first person in my family to get any college degree, much less a doctorate. I relate to them how my fears drove me to take important steps to make certain I did not fall behind in my work. I also attempt to convey that emotion of fear in hopes that some of them who are anxious may channel that anxiety in productive ways. Does it always work? No. But it is more effective than telling them to just try harder.

Finally, be patient, because active listening is hard work. You may be emotional at the moment you are speaking, and that is okay. Often we are dealing with emotional topics and we cannot get away from that reality. But we must have some patience for the person trying to understand our perspective. They are not in our head and words are an imperfect form of communication. They also are dealing with psychological barriers and biases interfering with their ability to process what we are stating. Be willing to provide a little grace if they are honestly struggling to comprehend your point of view. There are ways we can do a better job communicating our concerns to others. Our role as a communicator is as serious as our role as a listener. Hopefully we will consistently look at finding ways to improve in that role.

WHAT MUTUAL ACCOUNTABILITY LOOKS LIKE IN PROBLEM SOLVING

A fair question to ask is what this model looks like in solving racialized problems. How does it help us find solutions that move us closer to dealing with our history of racial abuse in a fair manner? Mutual accountability is not just an approach to constructing better interracial relationships; it also helps us engage in the problem solving we so desperately need in our society. If all we do is improve interpersonal relationships between racial groups, while laudable, that falls far short of the promise of this approach.

Several years ago Michael Emerson and I (2010) talked about a systematic way we can use the skills of active listening and awareness of the effects of group interest to solve racialized problems in our society. We theorized five steps that could be taken as part of a mutual accountability approach to problem solving. These steps have not been fully empirically tested, but they are supported by research on what it takes to build consensus. The steps we argue should be taken are

1. Define the racial problem.

2. Identify what we have in common.

3. Recognize our cultural or racial differences.

4. Create solutions that answer the concerns of the racial outgroup.

5. Find a compromise solution that works best for all.

Our first step is to clearly define which racial problems we want to address. We all can think of times when we started a discussion on one issue and then jumped around to so many other matters that we never solved the first issue that concerned us. There are many manifestations of our racialized society. If we try to solve them all at once, we will likely solve none of them. We must keep our conversation and effort focused on one issue at a time. Ideally, once we learn how to solve one racialized issue, we will learn how to solve other problems. Building momentum can be vital as success begets success through increased confidence in our ability to work across racial lines.

The next step is to identify what we have in common with those with whom we disagree. Obviously there are clear differences between racial groups or we would not be looking at a racialized problem. But it is also important to remember that we share some common values and concerns. Finding agreement can help us start a meaningful conversation. Research has indicated that recognizing where we agree can help us avoid unproductive conflict (Paulus, 2006). Recognizing areas of consensus is likely to lead to further agreements in our discussions with each other. That can be an important starting point for our conversation since it helps us build the trust we need to work together. Furthermore, recognizing what we have in common can help us forge a common identity that allows for more collaboration. What individuals agree on can vary depending on the issue being discussed. Agreement may be based on similar goals or values shared between the groups. Perhaps we can build on those elements. The key is that before we start looking at our disagreements, we should first identify our agreements.

Third, we come to the point where we recognize our differences and the contrasting arguments we use to support our perspectives. We must be honest about why we have our concerns. Pointing out how those perspectives have developed is important so that all parties have a chance to understand our points of contention. This is where active listening becomes even more important. Listening for understanding rather than for argument is key so that we fully understand the issues that separate us from those of other racial and political perspectives. It is also important that we concentrate on communicating with each other. Talking in ways that allow the hearer to comprehend what we are saying will go a long way in helping us find solutions that address real problems. It is also vital that all sides have an opportunity to articulate their concerns. If only one group gets to pronounce its vision for solving a racialized problem, then we are not doing collaborative communication. We are doing indoctrination. At the end of this stage all groups involved in the discussion should have a clear understanding of the concerns of the other groups. Learning to take the perspective of others is a valuable step in softening our hardness toward them (Lindsey, King, Hebl, & Levine, 2015) and making our interactions ripe for productive outcomes.

The next step is for us to create solutions that answer the concerns of our outgroup. If all we want to do is tell others our perspectives and expect them to agree with us, our conversations will quickly break down, becoming a tug-of-war to see who is more powerful. But if we have been actively listening, we can articulate others' concerns and address those concerns as well as our own. We may not arrive at a complete solution, but at least we can take a step in the right direction. Our ideas must not be merely theoretical either. They must be real solutions that move the ball forward.

Most individuals are in harmony with their own self-interest enough that they will not offer a solution that does not meet their own needs. But those who engage in active listening understand the other side's needs as well. This helps all parties recognize what is most important to them and what can be sacrificed to gain precious compromise. Often those motivated by colorblindness are concerned about equality and those motivated by antiracism are concerned about justice. Can we find solutions that combine both legitimate concerns? Can we fashion win-win solutions rather than win-lose outcomes?

Finally, we move to the last step, which is to find the compromise solution that best addresses the needs of all parties. Sometimes the compromise offered by one group looks like the compromise offered by the other. When that happens, it is relatively easy to construct a solution everyone supports. But at other times the plans conflict so dramatically that easy agreement is not possible. Ideally, because we have been attempting to address the concerns of others, our solutions at this stage of the dialogue are more similar than our opening positions. We should have moved closer to each other even if we are not yet in agreement. It may not be easy to come up with a compromise everyone can live with, but with the work we have put into our collaborative conversation, we are in a far better position to find those compromises than when the process started. Furthermore, we will have developed a level of trust and shared identity that will motivate us to keep working toward solutions. No one will get everything they want, but hopefully all will receive enough that they can accept and support the solution. Those are the win-win solutions we can use as bricks to build our pathway away from the insanity of racial alienation.

Let's use a hypothetical situation. Imagine a controversy focused on educational spending in a school district with a predominantly white school and a predominantly racial minority school. People of color may resent extra funding going to a gifted and talented program at the predominantly white school when their own school has no such program. Members of both parties may find agreement in their desire to increase the educational scores of all students in the district, which will help the overall reputation of both schools. But they recognize their differences in that whites want more focus on increasing the scores of their school while people of color want more focus on increasing the scores of their school.

As a possible solution, whites may propose a pilot program in the racial minority school in addition to keeping their own program. People of color may offer a solution where the program is set up at their school and students at the white school can be bused over to participate in that program. Finally, a compromise may be settled on where smaller programs are set up at both schools with the promise of growth as funds permit in coming years. I do not offer this hypothetical scenario to suggest that finding such compromises will be easy but to show how this model can potentially be applied in a real-world situation.[2]

The value of a mutual accountability approach is not limited to solving racialized problems. If we take this approach seriously, our entire lifestyle should be different, with us prioritizing collaborative communication over conflict. We should be looking at a larger movement that promotes these ideals far beyond the coercive pressures of colorblindness and antiracism. It has the potential to help us in many areas of our polarized society. I would be happy to see more productive conversations replace many of the political struggles and cultural wars that have cursed us for too long. In the last two chapters of this book, I will explore the larger implications of a broader mutual accountability approach. My focus will remain on how we can consider mutual accountability for racial issues, but it is clear that this is an idea that can revolutionize many other elements in our society.

OBJECTIONS TO MUTUAL ACCOUNTABILITY

Over the years I have discussed this model with many individuals. Some have loved it and some have found it interesting. But it does attract its share of critics. Not surprisingly the critics tend to be proponents of either colorblindness or antiracism. Among those who advocate colorblindness are individuals who question the need to even talk about racialized issues. They believe that people of color are either mistaken in their concerns or that those concerns are exaggerated, contending that we do not have a significant level of racism in our society. Some question the existence of

institutional discrimination and see discussion of this concept
as a way for people of color to induce guilt in whites. Many
admit that individual racists do exist in society, but they believe those individuals are few in number and do not have
much power. So in their view, paying attention to the way our
racialized society impacts people of color creates discord for
no reason. They see promotion of interracial communication
as efforts to gin up racial conflict. When I have tried to explain
that we cannot simply ignore racial issues and hope they go
away, they look at me as if I am the real racist. If people like
me would just shut up and concentrate on treating all people
the same, we would have a better society.

While I suspect that some of this disagreement is due to a
desire to hide from the negative effects of a racialized society,
it would not be fair for me to dismiss these arguments as dis-
ingenuous. At least some individuals truly do not see a
problem with institutional issues. They believe racism exists
only if those social institutions were created with the express
intent of depriving people of color of their rights. Institutions
do not need to intend to mistreat people of color in order to
discriminate against them. But for many with a colorblind
mentality, intention is key to determining whether racism is
a problem. For the person of color who has been deprived of
a job or serves a longer sentence because of institutional bias,
does it really matter if that institution was specifically designed to discriminate against them?

I challenge individuals loyal to colorblindness to ask themselves if they can truly know what it feels like to be in a marginalized group. Even if they are a person of color, it is worth

asking whether their individual experience is adequate for understanding how other people of color experience our racialized society. I hope those who espouse colorblindness can have the humility to realize that ignoring our racialized society simply does not work for those of us who have had to deal with the effects of racism in our lives. If they are willing to listen to the experiences of people of color and look at research with an open mind, I suspect they will realize we cannot be blind to the effects of racism. We must combat those effects and walk beside those who have suffered from them.

Some voices in the politically conservative world feed into a colorblind attitude in an unhealthy way. I have seen individuals take a single study and point out its weaknesses, as if by doing so they are eviscerating the entire notion of institutional bias. But that is not how science works. Science is not built on a single study but on a family of studies that create a framework by which we can understand social reality. Support for the existence of subtle prejudice and institutional discrimination comes from hundreds if not thousands of studies. Be wary of those who cherry-pick studies in an effort to undermine institutional bias. It is fine to question scientific findings, but understand that those who work in these areas of inquiry generally have read through much of the literature in their field and are not hanging their hat on a single study.

I am not saying those with a colorblind perspective must be quiet. It does no good to try to shut people up because you disagree with them. I want to hear from those with a colorblind perspective. They may be able to show me realities I normally do not see from my social position as an African

American man. I need those voices if I am going to be able to work toward solutions that serve the greatest number of people. But those individuals also need to listen to my voice and the voices of other people of color so they do not short-change the need to protect people of color. My invitation is not for those advocating for colorblindness to listen to a monologue but to invite them into a dialogue.

At the other end of the spectrum are those who advocate for antiracism. They also assert that there are certain principles that brook no argument or even discussion. Some antiracists argue that it is unfair to expect people of color, who have long been victimized by whites, to enter into an equitable conversation with those whites. They say the emotional burden people of color feel—a burden whites do not carry—is too much to bear during such a conversation. I have heard activists of color tell whites interested in racial issues to go read certain books rather than engaging in dialogue with them. The barriers to a mutual accountability approach erected by antiracism go beyond our general unwillingness to consider that we may be wrong. They also include an argument that it is unjust to expect people of color to engage in these conversations because of the pain such conversations will create.

I reject such an approach to dialogue. I do not deny there is emotional pain involved in entering into difficult conversations. But we must hold those conversations anyway if we want to engage in the moral suasion necessary to deal with racial alienation. I do not disagree that in some ways people of color bear more of the emotional burden than whites. Whites usually do not have the same level of investment in a need for social change. In a sense it is not fair to expect people of color to put their hearts into a conversation that whites can so easily dismiss. But we must decide just how badly we want things to change. Refusing to enter a discussion or sending people to read books simply will not have the impact of a conversation with a friend or even an acquaintance if that conversation is part of a collaborative communication effort.

Ultimately claims that people of color do not have to enter into productive mutual conversations with whites are counterproductive. I know that some racial minorities are not in the mood for compromise and working with others. They may calculate that they can win the political and cultural fight to get what they want. They may be able to shame some individuals into accepting what they want without an effort at collaborative communication. Okay— then what? If you win political battles and take what you want from others, they will not just go away. They will fight against you with all their might until the reforms or revolutions you have inspired fail. The backlash will inevitably come, because those who disagree with the social changes you have implemented have no investment in making those changes work. Maybe you can get nearly 100 percent of what you demand through political struggle, but it will be temporary. On the other hand, you can get 70 to 80 percent of what you desire through active listening and working with other people who will help instead of hinder you. That 70 to 80 percent will be sustainable if we pull together as a group across racial and ideological lines. The practical smart play is to engage in active listening to work out win-win solutions if what we want is long-term success.

Finally, I have heard some who promote antiracism complain because they think I am being too nice to whites. I find that to be an interesting complaint. It is as if niceness were a vice and we can have too much of it. I honestly wonder about those who complain about people of color being too nice to whites. Is the purpose to create a fair society or to punish modern whites for our society's centuries of racial abuse? We must focus on efforts to create a racially fair society rather than on any notion of punishment.

Some who feel I am too nice may be worried that my arguments provide aid and comfort to whites. Some whites may twist my words to argue that we do not need to address the concerns of people of color. Perhaps by arguing that people of color should listen to the concerns of whites, some will use my work to center the concerns of whites over the concerns of people of color. It is possible that my work will be misused, but the same can be said about anybody's work. Cannot complaints about the policing of people of color be distorted to justify violence against police officers? We must look at a fair interpretation of what is said rather than how someone may distort our words. Any fair reading of my work will indicate that it is not about centering the concerns of whites. It is about considering their perspective along with the perspectives of others.

I do not have a problem of being too nice. I have no problem talking to whites about institutional discrimination. I have no problem talking to whites about injustice in our racialized society. I have no problem talking to whites about their responsibility in doing what they can to make our society fairer for people of color. I do so in this book and my other writings. I have done these things in dozens, maybe hundreds, of conference speeches over the years and in my race and ethnicity courses. Being "nice" does not mean I will not provide whites with my honest interpretation of racial issues and their responsibility in making changes.

But what I will not do is dehumanize them and tell them they have no say in how we will progress in race relations. I will not treat them harshly because I may be able to get away with it due to feelings of white guilt. Because I have chosen not to take that path, I often can get them to let down their guard and get through to them in ways that antiracism simply cannot accomplish. The path toward ending racial alienation cannot include efforts to alienate racial outgroups, although at times we have to confront them. I will not participate in that approach, and if that makes me "too nice," so be it.

CONCLUSION

A mutual accountability model is about finding win-win solutions. Instead of focusing on getting everything we can get, we focus on what we need so we can work together instead of against each other. The difference between this model and a colorblindness or antiracism model is the focus on healthy interracial communications. In other models we are asked to accept preordained answers. A mutual accountability model assumes we cannot know the answers to our racialized problems until we have engaged in collaborative conversations with each other. When individuals are convinced they already have the right answers, they feel justified using legal, political, and cultural power to enforce those answers. Such expressions of power make racial alienation worse. But collaborative conversations emphasize moral suasion rather than power. The focus is on community building rather than winning the racial war.

There are times when the principles of both colorblindness and antiracism should be utilized. When I grade my students' papers, I am colorblind. I will not provide extra points for students from marginalized populations. They earn the grade according to their efforts and abilities. To do otherwise is to give them a distorted view of what they have learned. From antiracism we can learn how racism manifests itself in contemporary society even when that racism is not overt or intentional. The perspectives we can learn from antiracism are invaluable if we are going to identify manifestations of institutional discrimination and modern forms of prejudice. There are tools within both colorblindness and antiracism that we should use. But the focus of these models on gaining racialized victories against their social outgroups will continue to make them less effective than collaborative conversations to repair our damaged race relations.

Win-lose approaches pull our country apart. We need solutions that pull us together. That is the only way to develop sustainable pathways away from the racial alienation poisoning our society. We do not need more recrimination and name-calling. Victories gained by those techniques will face constant challenges and keep our society in turmoil. A great deal of the racial conflict in our society comes from our attempts to create benefit for those we support even if it is at the expense of those we do not support. I do not think individuals supporting those solutions want to harm others, but they simply do not care. They are focused on solutions that bring them comfort. If others bear the costs of those solutions, that is acceptable to them.

I cannot participate in such a game. The way forward is together. I have laid out my model of mutual accountability. As is true in all ideological concepts, there is not a final static form for this approach. But I hope what I have laid out here can be considered a starting point toward building a more comprehensive model.

THE REALITY OF INSTITUTIONAL DISCRIMINATION

STEVEN IS A WHITE PROFESSIONAL who works at a cancer center. He grew up in the suburbs in a predominantly white community. His best friend growing up was an immigrant from Vietnam. Although they were of different races, they did not talk much about racial issues. Steven did notice some of the ways whites treated Asians. And he himself was twice physically attacked by Asian immigrants, one of whom made a racist comment during the assault. These attacks did not make him angry at Asian immigrants since he had grown up around this community and Asians had also come to his defense. It did, however, reinforce to him that there were good and bad people in racial groups. Basically, he felt that people needed to get over racial issues.

When he went to college Steven became part of a ministry that started an outreach to Asian Americans. Some of the leaders of this outreach were Asian Americans who began to express hatred toward whites. This shocked Steven, who thought this attitude was ridiculous and unbecoming of Christian leaders. Not long after that, he was attending a Maori dance performance at his church when he overheard some angry comments from blacks who saw whites as oppressors. This frustrated him because he thought Christians should exhibit the love of Christ. These events in Steven's college years helped him draw certain conclusions about racial issues. Seeing self-segregation as a major barrier to meaningful conversation between the races, he thought people needed to get over it and stop avoiding each other. They did not need to assimilate or get rid of their culture, but on the other hand they did not need to hold their ethnicity as superior either.

Several events initiated a transformation in Steven's perspective on race. First was the shooting of Trayvon Martin in 2012. Second was the killing of Michael Brown two years later. Feeling grief at these deaths, Steven realized there were real issues of racial prejudice and policing that needed to be addressed. His grandfather, a police officer, had told him racial profiling was necessary for good police work. Now Steven wondered about the effects of that profiling in the African American community. As the narratives of Martin and Brown unfolded, he saw that the facts of the stories were different from how they originally appeared. Steven feared that these narrative changes would harden attitudes on both sides. People would look at the issues and simply react, unable to talk to each other because they didn't have words to communicate. Rather than taking in new information, people would stick to the narrative they wanted. In other words, whites would refuse to recognize the validity of what the black community was saying about police, and people of color would reject new information as it was revealed in these cases.

Seeing a failure on both sides to use language that was not fully adversarial, Steven grew more concerned. People used words such as *racism* in different ways. He knew of a college vice president who confessed to his own racism yet still passed a code of conduct indicating that any kind of racist action would lead to termination. Clearly the vice president was using different definitions for the word *racist*. Steven contended that this confusion was partly why people could not have productive conversations with each other. The meaning of words changed depending on the context and who used them. Finding common ground was becoming much more difficult.

However, Steven had a great opportunity to participate in real, meaningful conversations because he was interracially married. His conversations with his wife changed dramatically after George Floyd's murder. She talked to Steven about how tough life can be for people of color and how oppression can be informal and subtle. These conversations were tense at first but became easier over time. They helped him become more empathetic toward people of color. Today, if he could, Steven would tell his younger self that he needed to be more understanding and make fewer attempts to impose rationality onto his interactions with people of color. These conversations also helped Steven see how his being white could blind him to the realities sometimes faced by oppressed people groups.

Steven started out with a perspective that the best way to deal with race was to ignore it. But events shook his confidence in a colorblind approach and he ultimately rejected it. Steven also saw the tendencies of antiracism to suppress conversation as problematic as well. He eventually found himself advocating for common terms to be used in healthy interracial communication as the best way to foster the conditions necessary to solve racial problems in our society. Steven's journey away from colorblindness began with the shooting of African American men. Those shootings caused him to question whether society is fair to African Americans. That is a question that challenges a colorblind perspective.

THE DEFENSE OF COLORBLINDNESS

The worst legal thing you can be called today is a racist. It would be worse to be called a child molester, but child molestation is illegal. If I suspect someone is molesting his or her child, I need to call the police. If someone is engaging in racism, I do not call the police. It is not against the law to be a racist. But being labeled as racist comes with a powerful stigma and, depending on one's occupation, can even lead to unemployment. I can think of nothing worse to call someone without then having to call the police.

Because overt personal racism is so stigmatized today, there is a temptation to assume we have completely won the battle over racism. There is nothing left to do but enjoy a society where one's race no longer matters. The belief that colorblindness is the direction we should go is clear in the many conversations one hears in social media and on cable television. Surprisingly, there is not nearly as much support for this perspective in written form, such as blogs, online articles, and books, as there is for antiracism. I can only speculate about why. It may be that there is more societal support for antiracism than colorblindness.

It is also plausible—and I think this speculation is more likely to be accurate—that those with the cultural power are vastly more likely to promote antiracism than colorblindness. This explanation suggests that we have a divided society whereby those with social and cultural power who favor antiracism are pitted against those with a great deal less social and cultural power who favor colorblindness. According to the 2016 American National Election Studies survey, 56 percent of individuals believe blacks should work their way toward success without any special favors and 76 percent are against preferential hiring or promotion of blacks. While these questions are not exact measures of colorblindness, they do suggest that this ideology is relatively popular and that the popularity of colorblindness rivals that of antiracism.

Still, while material written by supporters of colorblindness is sparse, it does exist. One such supporter is Hughes (2019), who connects support of a colorblind perspective to the work of Martin Luther King, indeed calling King a "colorblind radical." While characterization of King as a supporter of colorblindness has been challenged by scholars (Polletta & Maresca, 2021; Turner, 1996; Yanco, 2014), it is helpful to see how King can be used to justify this perspective. According to Hughes, King focused on recruiting individuals across the racial spectrum to support his movement and wanted individuals evaluated for their character instead of their race. Hughes illustrates an important tenet of colorblindness in that individual efforts should determine how people are rewarded or punished. This leads to an opposition of any efforts seen as favoring people of color since such favors come at the expense of whites.

MacDonald (2018) argues that efforts to create opportunities for people of color result in a diluting of educational standards. The result is admission of unprepared college students. Furthermore, she contends that students of color who manage to make it through college are lower performers in their occupations and that other racial groups, notably Asian Americans, suffer from a loss of opportunity due to unfair affirmative action practices. She links the academic failures of marginalized racial groups to a culture of underachievement and a lack of adequate preparation for higher education. MacDonald's work concludes that a colorblind America is a fair America. Her argument reveals that colorblindness works as a fair system only if we can believe that the United States is a racially fair country.

McWhorter (2009) has also argued against efforts to provide racialized benefits to people of color. He questions the extent to which people of color are impacted by racism. His work reveals another important aspect of colorblindness: advocates generally believe that the impact of racism has been overblown by race scholars. They do not deny that racism exists, but they generally see it as a series of isolated incidents rather than a systemic problem. This is in keeping with a belief that our society is generally fair with a few disturbed racists who pop up their heads now and again. These few racists are almost always instantly marginalized in a country that rejects racism. In such a fair society, any efforts to aid blacks and Hispanics will inevitably negatively impact other racial groups, transforming a fair society into an unfair society.

The key sticking point with those advocating a colorblind perspective is the question of the degree to which we have overcome the effects of racism. If the effects of racism are relegated to a few racist individuals, then perhaps efforts to be colorblind can reflect our basically fair society. However, if there are still powerful effects from historical and contemporary racism that affect people of color beyond the hatred of a few racists, then colorblindness is not viable.

HOW OUR HISTORY STILL IMPACTS US —RESIDENTIAL SEGREGATION

Sometimes we ignore what got us where we are today. History is not just dry facts on a page in a textbook. Our history concerns real people and the experiences of those people, which helped establish our current social situation. There is a temptation to look at our society and ask, "What's the problem?" There is no race-based slavery in the United States. There are no internment centers. We punish people for being racists. So why do we need to consistently bring up the bad acts of yesterday?

The reality is that we will not truly understand our contemporary racial dilemma until we get a handle on historical abuse and how that abuse continues to manifest itself today.

Such an examination is complicated, and reams of books have been written about the way historical racism impacts us today. I want to keep this as simple as possible, so I will look at a single issue of how racial history has impacted the lives of people of color and use that as an illustration of the larger trend. That issue will be residential segregation.

Historically our society has enacted racist laws and customs that trapped people of color into segregated neighborhoods. Native Americans were forced into reservations. Asian Americans were driven into ethnic enclaves. African Americans in the South were not allowed to live among whites due to Jim Crow restrictions. In the North, the establishment of ghettos limited where African Americans could reside. Indeed today, there is more residential segregation in the Northeast than the South. Similar social pressure kept Hispanic Americans in barrios, especially those in the lower economic classes.

Residential segregation is a common story in the history of people of color. And it did not happen by accident. Governmental policies inhibited people of color from obtaining homes in integrated neighborhoods. Social custom discouraged people of color from living among whites. The final barrier was violence carried out by white supremacist groups, who terrorized any people of color who dared try to live among whites.

These historical realities set into motion mechanisms that tend to keep us residentially segregated today. Hispanic and Asian Americans become notably less segregated as they move up in class, but blacks tend to remain segregated even at

higher income levels. One of the primary reasons this segregation remains beyond historical tradition is that whites are
less willing to move to black neighborhoods (Emerson, Chai,
& Yancey, 2001). There is no doubt our historical patterns
have helped set up the racial segregation we see today. Our
current residential segregation is not just a matter of ingroup
preference. While ingroup racial preference for neighbors is
true for all racial groups, research indicates that whites are
less willing to live with those of other races than people of
color (Howell & Emerson, 2018; Krysan, Couper, Farley, &
Forman, 2009; Krysan & Farley, 2002). A combination of historical patterns and contemporary racial preference is what
drives residential segregation today.

The residential segregation established by historical racism
comes at a significant cost for people of color. The fact that
minorities are segregated into different areas of the city
makes certain types of discrimination possible. Redlining is
the practice whereby financial lenders designate minority
and racially mixed neighborhoods as poor investment areas.
As a result residents in those areas receive fewer and smaller
loans than those living in white neighborhoods. The redlining
made possible by neighborhood segregation is one of the
ways financial institutions mistreat people of color. A study by
the Federal Reserve Board in 1991 showed that white bor-
rowers with the lowest incomes were approved for mortgages
more easily than financially well-off people of color (Knight,
1991). This difference persisted whether the mortgages were
sought from local banks, the Federal Housing Administration,
or the Veterans Administration. The discrimination people

of color face in lending is exacerbated by the reality of racial residential segregation. And that discrimination has not significantly decreased over the last few decades (Anyaso, 2020).

There is another cost to segregation: the separation of lower-class minorities from the resources they need to improve their lives. Poorer minorities are less likely to have transportation to get to work. It is not an accident that they are not able to reach more prosperous white neighborhoods easily (Massey & Denton, 1993; Quillian, 2002). Furthermore, they may not have a decent choice of stores from which to buy food. The few stores that are in the neighborhood are free to overcharge minority residents. I remember doing research on multiracial churches in a city that was segregated by a river that ran through the city. The black area of town made up about one-third of the city. Yet in a city of about fifty thousand individuals, there was only one grocery store in the black section of town. This is not an unusual situation for neighborhoods made up of people of color. Whites in mostly white neighborhoods will not be affected by this lack of resources and may have little incentive to correct the situation.

Attending high school in Amarillo, Texas, I remember feeling the effects of that lack of resources. I lived in a predominantly black neighborhood. There were few businesses close to where I lived. To get a job in high school, and before I could drive a car, I had to catch a bus to go across town. It generally took about an hour for me to get to work. Then about an hour to get back home. Yes, I was able to obtain a job. I was not denied the job outright because of my race. But it cost me two extra hours almost every shift because I did not live in the predominantly white areas of the city. Had there been businesses close by, I would have been able to obtain money without such a drain on my time.

A final cost of segregation is the concentration of many dysfunctional elements in lower-class communities of color. Douglas Massy and Nancy Denton in their classic book *American Apartheid* (1993) indicate that African Americans are especially likely to live in conditions of extreme residential segregation. They argue that within black neighborhoods there is a concentration of individuals who are jobless, potential criminals, pregnant as teenagers, or otherwise experiencing those factors found more frequently among the poor than the wealthy. The concentrated poverty of poorer minorities means these dysfunctions are not spread to different communities and the toxicity of these effects are magnified within communities of color.

Here is how this works out in our society. We clearly have poor white neighborhoods that suffer from many of the same problems we find in poor communities of color. Whites living in poverty experience the concentration of crime, broken families, poor schools, and drugs that are so often a problem in poor neighborhoods. But if whites can gain economic resources, they can move away from poor neighborhoods and protect their families from many of these deleterious effects. Residential segregation makes it harder for people of color to remove themselves from such neighborhoods. Thus, to stay in a neighborhood of color is to stay much closer to the negative elements of poverty, even for a family of color that has reached middle-class status. This problem is particularly hard on African Americans, as middle-class blacks are less likely to live in integrated neighborhoods than the middle classes among other people of color.

People of color pay the price for the historical racism we have experienced in the United States. Residential segregation is only one example of the impact of historical racism; there are other ways people of color pay the price. For instance, a well-demonstrated wealth gap is also tied to historical disadvantages (Shapiro, Meschede, & Osoro, 2013). Our school system feeds off residential segregation, which multiplies the disadvantages of people of color (Quillian, 2014). The medical shortcomings that plague people of color likely contribute to higher rates of mortality and morbidity (Paradies, Truong, & Priest, 2014; Prather, Fuller, Marshall, & Jeffries IV, 2016).

History matters. Until we recognize this, we are unlikely to understand why people of color economically fail at higher rates than whites and why some of them are still angry over historical racism.

INSTITUTIONAL DISCRIMINATION

The issues we must address are not limited to historical racism. People of color face contemporary institutional barriers as well. You have probably heard of the concept of institutional racism, or discrimination. It can be defined as those mechanisms that lead to racial inequality regardless of whether there was intent to do so. If we want to rid ourselves of racial inequality, it makes sense to identify and eliminate institutional discrimination.

Of course, some systems lead to differential impacts that we do not want to eliminate. For example, since African Americans are more likely, even after controls for individual characteristics, to commit murder (O'Flaherty & Sethi, 2010), one could argue that laws against murder are examples of institutional discrimination. Given the historical effects of racism, this is undoubtedly true. Historical racism likely has made murder more commonplace in the African American community than in the European American community. But for obvious reasons we should not rid ourselves of laws against murder. What we would lose from eliminating those laws far outweighs any benefit we would get from ending this racial disparity.

But if this is institutional discrimination and discrimination is wrong, how can I argue that it is okay to outlaw murder? This question assumes that racism is always a result of personal animosity, and this is not the case with institutional discrimination. Mechanisms that disproportionately affect people of color do not need to be motivated by racial animosity. This objection fails to take into consideration the definition of institutional discrimination.

Second, murder laws are a great illustration of how we can have just laws that are implemented unjustly. I am not saying African Americans engage in murder at the same rates as European Americans. I accept the research that states otherwise. I am arguing that the way we adjudicate those laws is often far from fair. Research (Cox, 2009; Free, 1996; Lurigio & Loose, 2008; Mitchell, 2005) indicates that, all things being equal, blacks are more likely to be arrested, charged, convicted, and receive longer sentences than whites. We know that the killing of whites, especially by blacks, makes it more likely for a criminal to receive the death penalty (F. Baumgartner, 2016; Holcomb, Williams, & Demuth, 2004). Even as we acknowledge that murder laws disproportionately impact African Americans even when fairly applied, we also need to be realistic in looking at the biases in our society that contribute to unfair treatment.

I point out murder laws because I know that when I talk about institutional discrimination, some will argue that there are rules and laws in place that may result in discrimination but that we must keep. I accept that reality, although keeping those rules and laws does not relieve us of the responsibility to implement them fairly. Nor does it relieve us of the responsibility to look at the root of the differences in the commission of this crime and try to deal with them. Are these differences tied to culture? Possibly. Are they tied to economic forces that make it harder for people of color to believe they will be treated fairly? It is naive to not consider that possibility.

But there are many ways in which institutional discrimination occurs that cannot be so easily defended. For example, although it is better than it was in the past, we still have serious sentencing disparities for those who use crack and those who use powder cocaine (Morris, 2014). Since African Americans are more likely than European Americans to use crack cocaine, blacks tend to serve longer sentences than whites. It does not matter whether there is a racist intent behind this disparity. The results are unfair for people of color. This is the common form of institutional discrimination:

unfair outcomes due to mechanisms that are not easily justified. Given that crack and powder cocaine are basically the
same drug, it is problematic that they are treated differently.

Let's look at an example outside of criminal justice.
Sometimes businesses hire by word of mouth. That is, when
they need to find someone for a position, they ask their
employees if they know anyone who needs a job and is a
good worker. The thinking is that if someone can vouch for
a potential employee, the chances that this person will be
a good fit with the company are fairly high. There is a
certain logic to this approach. This hiring strategy does not
indicate that someone is a racist. But our social networks
tend to be made up of people like us. One of the ways they
are like us is race. If whites are more likely to be in positions
of occupational power, they are more likely to find white
employees from their social networks. As a result, whites
can gain jobs people of color never even knew were open.
The employer may have had no intention of being racist.
But the result is still an unfair advantage for whites over
people of color.

We could explore many more examples of institutional
discrimination. We could look at transportation systems that
make it harder for people of color to get to resources
(Bullard, Johnson, & Torres, 2004; Golub, Marcantonio, &
Sanchez, 2013), educational funding that denies people of
color the same educational opportunities as whites (Alemán
Jr., 2007; Walters, 2001), or political systems that minimize
the votes of people of color (Combs, 2016; Slocum & Lee,
2004). Many research articles and books have been written

that lay out the ways institutional discrimination impacts people of color. My purpose is not to rehash these examples but to indicate that this type of discrimination is real and something we must deal with if we want a fair society. Historical racism has produced a significant amount of institutional discrimination, and we are still feeling the effects of that discrimination today.

I understand that whites can become frustrated during conversations about institutional discrimination since this form of racism does not necessarily result from anyone's personal bias against other races. But this is not about personal blame. The sooner we can get away from the attribution of personal guilt, the easier it will be to accept the reality of these structural forces and move forward to deal with them. I would ask whites to look at institutional discrimination from the point of view of a person of color who is either serving a longer than fair sentence or not getting a job due to factors beyond his or her control. Problematic institutional measures are not easily recognized, and their invisibility makes them all the more sustainable in a society that stigmatizes overt racism. Institutional discrimination does more damage to people of color today than white supremacist groups. White supremacists are largely rejected in our society, but mechanisms that support institutional discrimination are generally accepted. I have no need to make personal accusations toward whites or to try to make whites feel guilty. But I do want my white brothers and sisters to work with me for a fairer society where we confront and challenge institutional discrimination wherever we find it.

DO WE STILL HAVE PERSONAL RACIAL BIAS?

Although overt racism is highly stigmatized today, we still should question whether racial bias within individuals still exists. In focusing on institutional issues, it may seem that I have overlooked the role of personal—even if subtle—racial bias. I have not. There is still prejudice against people of color that may be unconscious or may be blatant. Either way, it is real and racial minorities can feel its effects.

For example, we know that in the past twenty-five years racial discrimination in hiring has not really decreased at all (Quillian, Pager, Hexel, & Midtbøen, 2017). In what are known as audit studies, researchers send in job applications signaling that the applicant is white (usually through use of a name such as Emily or Brad), that the applicant is black (once again through a name such as Latonya or Jermaine), or that the applicant is another racial minority (using a name such as Juan or Isabelle). The applicants' qualifications are basically the same. Several studies show that the white candidate is more likely to receive an invitation to interview than the racial minority candidate. This favoritism for white applicants has not decreased since the turn of the century. Discrimination against people of color is not a historical event. This discrimination persists today.

Need more evidence? The concept of "driving while black" is the tendency for African Americans to be pulled over by the police at higher levels than European Americans. There is statistical support for this concept (Harris, 2010). Research indicates that it is not an isolated incident—it is not just a rogue sheriff or police officer responsible for this type of discrimination. Harris looks at four areas in Ohio to support his argument that blacks are treated differently while behind the wheel. There is similar evidence in other areas of our country (F. R. Baumgartner, Christiani, Epp, Roach, & Shoub, 2017; F. R. Baumgartner, Epp, & Shoub, 2018). This discrepancy is likely tied to other problems African Americans face in our criminal justice system. If blacks are being pulled over more than whites, then white criminals have an easier time escaping punishment. This helps explain the fact that blacks are more likely to be arrested. The same dynamics that lead to more arrests may well lead to more convictions and longer sentences for African Americans. Differences in how often blacks are pulled over do not merely cause inconvenience but contribute to other disparities in law enforcement. When we take these factors into account, data showing that African Americans are more likely to be wrongly convicted than others in the US population is not surprising (Gross, Possley, & Stephens, 2017).

Finally, there is evidence of racism in the beliefs and practices of medical healthcare providers. Paradies, Truong, and Priest's (2014) work documents evidence of racism in twenty-six of the thirty-seven studies they examined. Some racism was found in the attitudes of healthcare workers who engaged in negative stereotyping and distancing themselves from people of color. Other research looked at differences in treatment people of color received relative to white patients. One study found that black women were less likely to be referred for cardiac catheterization. They also found evidence that healthcare personnel were less willing to trust racial minority patients. It does not take a great deal of imagination to see how lack of trust would affect the experience of people of color in our healthcare system.

There is strong evidence of ongoing disadvantages for people of color even in a society where overt racism is stigmatized. It is important to recognize this disadvantage and understand that this is not a claim that we still live under Jim Crow or a system that forced Native Americans onto reservations. At those times there were overt rules preventing the success of people of color. But subtle types of discrimination also construct barriers that make life harder for people of color.

IMPACT OF BARRIERS

Given the effects of historical racism, institutional bias, and subtle racial discrimination, it is fair to say that people of color face barriers whites do not. These barriers are not the same as they were in the past when people of color were legally forbidden to have success in school or at work. Rather, the barriers are hidden and not clearly observable. Nonetheless, their effects are real. Pretend we are going to have a mile-long race a year from now. I gather a group of people and tell a third of them about the race and hire a trainer for them. Six months later I tell another third of the group about the race. I do not hire them a trainer, but I do advise them to work on their own to get ready for the race. The final third of the group I call the morning of the race and tell them it is time to run.

Assuming the group is randomly divided in terms of ability, we know what will happen in the race, do we not? On average the first group will do the best, followed by the second group, with the third group having the worst times. There may be someone in the third group who is a natural miler and happened to be training on a consistent basis anyway. He may run a sub-four-minute mile and run away from everyone else. But he will be an anomaly. On average having a trainer and time to train means you will perform better. The fact that some individuals of color have enjoyed wild success does not mean institutional discrimination is a myth. It merely means some individuals have been able to overcome the barriers that inhibited them and society's distaste for overt racism allowed them to enjoy the fruits of that success.

If we simply showed up the day of the race to observe, we could rationally conclude that members of the first group were simply better athletes. Or maybe they worked harder than the rest. This is often what people say when they look at different economic or educational outcomes between racial groups. But the advantages of time and resources to train will be borne out over time in this competition. This is not a contest to see who is the superior athlete or hardest worker. Yes, it is possible to overcome disadvantages, but over time those disadvantages will ensure that, as a whole, one group will do better than the other two. This is how we need to understand the relative advantages and disadvantages tied to racial identity.

So if we are part of the first group and we show up for the race after a year of training and advantage, what should we do? Should we run the race as we planned and ignore our advantages? If we did that, would we not expect resentment from the members of the other two groups and strained relations between them and us? Perhaps we should seek out ways to make the race fair. Maybe we postpone the race or give members of the other groups some sort of head start. Of course, what members of the first group believe should happen to make the race fair is not likely what members of the other two groups will think. But this discussion must take place since we do not have a fair race.

THE FAILURE OF COLORBLINDNESS

I recently posted on Facebook about my desire to teach my sons about racial issues. Even though I have expertise in racial issues, I recognize that child rearing is a whole new world, and I wanted to solicit ideas from my friends who were raising kids of color on how to approach that challenge. I did receive some ideas, but I also got pushback. Some people were irritated that I thought I needed to talk about racial issues with my boys. In their minds it was an unnecessary conversation. I tried to explain that my boys had to become ready to deal with racial issues since they were of color, but that did not satisfy my critics. They argued that I should concern myself with raising good solid men. Bringing up racial issues simply added complication to that task.

When asked how to deal with historical racism in a fair manner, those who support colorblindness say the answer is to ignore race. They focus on making certain whites are not overly burdened with efforts to correct the effects of racial abuse. They are more willing to err on the side of protecting whites from the consequences of overcorrection of our racialized society than to not provide enough correction for the racial harms done to people of color. Some would argue that we need to go into communities of color and teach them how to be successful in our society. This type of Anglo-conformist mentality can provide help to people of color without truly acknowledging the toxic effects of historical racism and institutional bias. But ultimately there is a push among those who support colorblindness to shut down conversations about the continuing effects of racism.

In light of the evidence of historical racism, institutional discrimination, and contemporary prejudice, we should be skeptical about notions of colorblindness. This is not about the intentions or heart of those who push these ideals. Indeed, there is much to be desired in the idea that we move beyond the pain of past racism. It can be seductive to think that if we ignore our racial differences we will eliminate racial animosity. At one time I thought the best way to not be troubled by racism was simply to not be troubled by racism. Stop worrying about racial distinctions and everything will be okay. But my experiences with racism and prejudice have shown me that this is not a viable solution.

There is an unspoken danger in colorblindness that does not always get sufficient attention. A colorblind mentality causes intense frustration that builds up within people of color who live out the consequences of our racialized society. Many of us see the attitudes of such whites as uncaring at best and racist at worst. I think it is a mistake to link such attitudes to racism, but I understand the frustration. It is the sort of frustration that can lead some people of color to radicalize. This is what happens when people of color no longer care about the perspective of whites and adopt a harsh attitude toward anyone who does not fully support the tenets of antiracism. I understand the temptation to radicalize because I have felt such temptations myself. I've had conversations with whites who show not the slightest interest in the effects of racism unless we can show someone saying the N-word, even after I have defended them from unfair charges of racism. This makes me think I am wasting my time defending them. It tempts me to disregard any efforts to be fair and just look out for the interests of people of color. I fought off such temptations, knowing I would be of little good in creating the right atmosphere to deal with racial alienation if I became radicalized. Ultimately it is the responsibility of those of us of color to avoid radicalization so we can contribute to a healthy racial culture. But whites who ignore the persistent effects of racism are not helping us.[1]

Colorblindness does not describe our social reality. People of color are not making up stories about their experiences of racism. There are real issues to which they are reacting. To tell them to ignore not only the lasting effects of historical racism but also the continuing impact of institutional discrimination and contemporary prejudice is not realistic. Strident colorblindness is the type of threatening perspective many people of color cannot hear since we wonder how we can address racial unfairness if we do not even acknowledge it exists. We can't. So if we want to deal with racial alienation, we have to move beyond a colorblind approach.

We cannot ignore the history of racial abuse in the United States, for doing so would make the barriers people of color encounter permanent. Whites too often ignore brothers and sisters of color when we try to tell them about the disadvantages we face. I want whites to be aware that a colorblind framework that generally works for them creates frustration for people of color because it does not fit with our current reality. It is tempting for whites to say everything is okay, and from their point of view it probably is. But it is not okay for us, and as long as that is the case, we cannot be satisfied with the status quo. We can no longer deny the reality of the effects of historical racism, institutional discrimination, and contemporary subtle prejudice. We need reforms to address these issues.

WHY ANTIRACISM FAILS

AS OF EARLY 2021, Robin DiAngelo's 2018 book *White Fragility* was number one on the *New York Times* and Amazon nonfiction bestseller lists. Number two on the Amazon list was *How to Be an Antiracist* (Kendi, 2019). I cannot remember a time when two books so similar in topic topped the bestseller lists. Several other books have also helped popularize the concept of antiracism (Eddo-Lodge, 2020; Fidel, 2020; Kendall, 2021; Kivel, 2017; Oluo, 2019; Pollock, 2008).

In addition to these popular books, antiracism is having a major economic impact. Approximately eight billion dollars is spent every year on diversity training programs. Diversity training is mandated in almost all Fortune 500 companies and in nearly two-thirds of colleges and universities (Pan, 2020). I do not know what percentage of that eight billion dollars goes specifically to antiracism efforts, but given that trainers such as DiAngelo can command up to twenty thousand dollars for a talk (Soave, 2020) and Tim Wise receives between ten and twenty thousand (Speaker Booking Agency, 2020), it is naive to think that antiracists are not getting a good chunk of that money. The question is, Does antiracism improve race relations? If it does, then the money is well spent. If it does not, we are just throwing money down the drain. If it makes race relations worse, we are in a world of hurt.

WHAT IS ANTIRACISM?

What is wrong with being an antiracist? Nobody want to be a racist. Should we not all oppose racism and thus be antiracist? Of course we should all oppose racism. But the term *antiracism* means more than merely opposing racism. We must understand a few definitions first if we are going to grasp the lessons antiracism offers. We will look to the writings of antiracism supporters to gain an idea of the philosophy behind this term; however, those proponents disagree with each other. For example, Robin DiAngelo (2018) contends that blacks cannot be racists, but Ibran X. Kendi (2019) argues that blacks can be racist if they do not adopt antiracist beliefs. Clearly, this is not something antiracists agree on.

To attain the clearest understanding of antiracism possible, I looked through several books, online articles, and blogs that offered definitions of antiracism. The themes exhibited in those writings that go basically unchallenged by other antiracists will help us grasp the core shared beliefs. While just about any definition I offer will leave out someone who calls himself or herself an antiracist, this method will minimize the number of such individuals. I found three such concepts, even if they were represented in distinct ways, upon which to build a working definition of antiracism.[1]

The first concept concerns a belief in the pervasiveness of racism in our society. A common definition used by many antiracists and attributed to NAC International Perspectives: Women and Global Solidarity is that antiracism is "the active process of identifying and eliminating racism by changing systems, organizational structures, policies and practices and attitudes, so that power is redistributed and shared equitably." This definition reflects the multifaceted nature of racism the way antiracists see it. Racism is not merely overt racial hatred (DiAngelo, 2018; Hoffower, 2021; Jewell, 2020; Saad, 2020) but is prevalent throughout our society (Fidel, 2020; Hoffower, 2021; Kendi, 2019; Pollock, 2008; Snyder, 2020). Some contend that we live in a system of white supremacy that continues to work to the advantage of whites (Jewell, 2020; Kivel, 2017; Oluo, 2019; Saad, 2020; Tomkin, 2020). While most whites may not overtly hate people of color, they condone a social system that works to their advantage. Antiracists believe whites have an obligation to renounce this evil system and work toward tearing it down. The degree to which antiracists perceive our society as poisoned by racism, white privilege, and white supremacy may vary, but the idea that racism is multifaceted and pervasive in our society is a theme found in most if not all of the antiracist readings I examined.

The second common concept among antiracists is the necessity of an intense commitment to defeat racism. Antiracism is a moral cause that individuals must take up even if it costs them greatly (Eddo-Lodge, 2020; Kendi, 2019; Oluo, 2019; Saad, 2020). It is not enough to be against racism in principle; we must be activists in our attempts to root it out of our society (Hoffower, 2021; Snyder, 2020). Kendi (2019) has famously argued that one cannot be a nonracist. One is either a racist or an antiracist. While other antiracists may not adopt this exact dichotomy, it is clear in their writings that they ask for intentional efforts to deal with racism and offer solutions within their antiracist framework on the type of actions to be taken. Antiracism is a philosophy that demands activism and criticizes individuals who choose to sit out the battle against racism.

The third common theme in antiracism is that the role of whites is to support the activism of people of color. Antiracists challenge whites to provide such support (DiAngelo, 2018; Eddo-Lodge, 2020; Kivel, 2017; Saad, 2020; Tomkin, 2020), while their communication to people of color is generally more sympathetic in tone (DiAngelo, 2018; Jewell, 2020; Oluo, 2019; Snyder, 2020). If this sounds like differential expectations for whites and nonwhites, that is because there are differential expectations for whites and nonwhites.

What is demanded of whites varies by author, although they almost all make explicit demands. One prominent antiracist requires whites to largely reject their white identity (DiAngelo, 2018). Others look to whites to develop humility in their interactions with people of color (Hoffower, 2021; Oluo, 2019; Saad, 2020). Whites are told to "preach" the virtues of antiracism to other whites (DiAngelo, 2018; Eddo-Lodge, 2020; Saad, 2020). There are calls for whites to provide financial support for people of color and their activism (Eddo-Lodge, 2020; Oluo, 2019; Tomkin, 2020) and to redistribute financial assets to people of color (Jewell, 2020; Kendi, 2019). Whites are to support antiracism without expecting anything in return or that they will have a significant leadership role in the antiracist movement (Eddo-Lodge, 2020; Jewell, 2020; Saad, 2020; Tomkin, 2020). There is a clear delineation between the roles of whites and nonwhites in that whites are expected to defer to nonwhites.[2]

These concepts provide an operational definition of antiracism as it is used in the general public. Antiracism is a strong, active commitment to remove multifaceted and systematic manifestations of racism with an emphasis on whites supporting the activism of people of color. This is the view consistently expressed in popularized antiracist material.

AN ASSESSMENT OF ANTIRACISM

I have concerns about antiracism. But those concerns are not connected to the first two themes in my definition: the pervasiveness of racism and the necessity to counteract it. In the last chapter I presented evidence of historical and institutional racism. Racism is a multifaceted problem we need to confront. We must be proactive in confronting this problem. Racism is a wound festering in the heart of this country. Wounds do not go away until we do something to heal them. We can argue about how proactive we should be, or what we should do to combat racism, but ignoring it is not an option. These two concepts fit well with a collaborative-conversations approach in that we need those conversations to be proactive to deal with the multifaceted nature of racism.

My problems with antiracism emerge with the third theme concerning the role of whites. In my mutual accountability model we are all at the table making decisions together. Whites are not put at a "kids' table" or limited to supporting only the ideas of people of color. Many in antiracism believe it is fair to restrict whites in this way because the voices of people of color have been silenced for so long. Philosophically, I struggle with the notion that we can move forward in society with such a two-tiered system. If it could be shown to work empirically, I could put away my concerns, but the antiracism books and articles I read rarely if ever provide evidence that these techniques actually work. Maybe that is because research suggests they do not work.

One of the common techniques used in antiracism is diversity training, which ideally convinces whites to become proactive antiracists. Diversity training has recently surged in popularity (Judkis, 2020); however, it has been shown to have little long-term effect on prejudice (Lai et al., 2016), and there is limited evidence that it furthers social justice outcomes (Alhejji, Garavan, Carbery, O'Brien, & McGuire, 2016). What's more, the implementation of diversity programs can convince majority group members that their organization's racial problems have been solved (Dover, Kaiser, & Major, 2020; Kaiser et al., 2013) and can even increase majority group bias against oppressed groups (Duguid & Thomas-Hunt, 2015; Heilman & Welle, 2006). Finally, whites on Christian college campuses developed less of an interest in fighting racism when they learned about antiracial programs on those campuses (Yancey, 2010). As a tool for promoting antiracism values, diversity training is suspect at best.

Of course, not all diversity programs are based on anti-racism principles. So it is useful to look specifically at programs that do involve those elements. For example, many antiracists emphasize the importance of whites learning about their privilege (DiAngelo, 2018; Kendi, 2019; Kivel, 2017; Oluo, 2019; Saad, 2020). This fits with the notion that whites should learn to be humble and challenge the advantages their whiteness brings about. However, teaching others about the prevalence of white privilege may do more harm than good since a focus on privilege can actually decrease sympathy for poor whites even as it fails to raise overall sympathy for poor blacks (Cooley, Brown-Iannuzzi, Lei, & Cipolli III, 2019). It can also motivate backlash from political conservatives and moderates (Brad, Spisz, & Tanega, 2019). Antiracism tends to emphasize the need to compel whites to learn from people of color, but research has indicated that forcing whites to undergo diversity training can generate backlash against people of color (Legault, Gutsell, & Inzlicht, 2011; Plant & Devine, 2001).

Some antiracists emphasize the need to redistribute resources (Eddo-Lodge, 2020; Kendi, 2019; Kivel, 2017; Tomkin, 2020). Yet justifications for racism remedies centered on redistribution of resources from whites to nonwhites can result in a resistance to those remedies (Kidder, Lankau, Chrobot-Mason, Mollica, & Friedman, 2004; Sanchez & Medkik, 2004). While we may not yet have a way to differentiate antiracism programs from other diversity programs, when we look at programs containing elements antiracists consider important, we find little evidence in their favor outside of isolated experiments (Guh, Harris, Martinez, Chen, & Gianutsos, 2019; Johnson, Antle, & Barbee, 2009)[3] that antiracism creates positive attitudinal and behavioral change.

Perhaps a longer period of education will eventually alter attitudes over time. In theory that seems possible, but it depends on how we educate individuals. One would think our education system, which has become more focused on teaching diversity and acceptance, would produce individuals who act less racist. But evidence shows this is not true. Education may tell us what to say to avoid being labeled a racist but it does not necessarily convince us to alter our actions. For example, educated whites are less likely to exhibit racism in their answers to questions about where they will send their kids to school, but they are less likely to send their kids to a racially integrated school than other whites (Sikkink & Emerson, 2008). Combining a skepticism that education creates significant attitudinal and behavior change with the research cited above indicating that antiracism training is not effective makes it hard to believe that long-term antiracism programs will be any more effective than short-term ones. We need something deeper if we are to create deep attitudinal and behavioral changes.

In my research, I was struck by how many articles and books written by antiracists are directed at whites and how whites need to change. There is a confrontational aspect to these writings that may reflect a confrontational element within antiracism. But what does it take to convince someone to adopt a different attitude? What does it take to bring about moral suasion? If we want to truly persuade individuals, there are a number of important actions we can take. We should identify where we agree with the person, admit when the other person has made a good point, build rapport, and understand the arguments that person has for his or her beliefs. If we can accomplish these goals, we have a chance to convince them of our point of view. This is how moral suasion works and when it is undertaken in such a manner, we can build community instead of intensifying division.

Does this sound like what happens in antiracism sessions? Do such proponents seek to understand the perspectives of those who disagree with them? Do they attempt to find areas of agreement? Do antiracists admit it when those they disagree with make a good point? When antiracists dismiss the perspectives of whites, they are not operating under the best practices for moral suasion. What happens when we tell whites they must comply with the desires of people of color? Do we find true allies or those who are afraid to speak their minds? By allowing others to speak their minds, we gain an opportunity to truly interact with them, learn their perspectives, and have hope that we can alter previous opinions. But when we attempt to stigmatize the ideas of others so they will accept our own ideas, we are using power. The research on persuasion suggests that the methodology of antiracism does not lead to real change but to compliance out of fear of being labeled a racist.

Finally, I want to investigate practical methods that arise out of antiracism. Antiracism should naturally lead to a desire to be proactive in working toward goals, one of which is hiring people of color in leadership roles. Such hiring can provide people of color access to power in ways they have been denied in the past. A proactive approach could be for a company to institute mandatory diversity training to bring awareness to hiring managers so that people of color have a better chance of gaining employment. Given the notion of a nation dominated by white supremacy, it is reasonable to ask businesses to change and create a better atmosphere for people of color. For instance, they could start utilizing employment tests so white managers will not simply hire from their white social networks or set up grievance systems to make sure people of color are treated right. There has been research (Dobbin & Kalev, 2016) on the efforts of companies to hire managers of color by exploring the use of mandatory diversity training, employment tests, and grievance systems. These researchers documented which companies used these tools and checked back five years later to see if the number of managers of color had increased. What they found was that the opposite had taken place. Five years later the companies that implemented these techniques had fewer managers of color in their ranks. It seems that implementing proactive programs designed to mandate racial inclusion can create the opposite of what antiracists desire.[4]

As a man of color, I understand the attraction of antiracism. I do not always trust whites to do the right thing when it comes to correcting the effects of historical racism and institutional discrimination. The purity of focus in antiracism makes sense when you consider how many individuals deny the importance of dealing with racism. But the solutions antiracism offers are unbalanced and do not work. Antiracism fails to be effective in lessening racial alienation, and it is not effective in achieving such goals as hiring managers of color. Part of me wants antiracism efforts to succeed, but they simply don't. I must choose whether I will feed that emotional part of myself that would like to use antiracism to put pressure on whites to confront racism or listen to empirical evidence showing that it has failed. I choose the latter.

Even though I am sympathetic to the aims of antiracism, it is a mistake to think it is attractive to all people of color. Research I conducted a while ago indicated that blacks are no more likely to accept the notion that blacks cannot be racist than whites (Yancey, 2005). Although we know not all antiracists believe that blacks cannot be racists, it is still a common belief in antiracism. But education is actually a better predictor of the belief that blacks cannot be racist than race is. Recent research (English & Kalla, 2021) also indicates that framing policy issues in racial ways does not produce more support among African Americans. Antiracism may be a philosophy more attractive to the highly educated than to people of color in general.

GROUP INTEREST THEORY AND ANTIRACISM

In addition to the lack of empirical support, there are also theoretical arguments against antiracism and its effectiveness in reducing racial alienation. Group interest theory (Katz & Taylor, 2013) is the idea that we are inclined to support ideas and engage in actions that favor people in our ingroups. We have a racial history in which whites abused people of color, and this has resulted in a contemporary system in which people of color are disadvantaged. Because of this history we have a powerful need to move from racialized institutions that work better for majority group members to systems that are fair for everybody. But our desire to act in ways that are good for our own group means we will favor institutional systems that help our group even at the expense of others. It is not surprising that whites are likely to favor maintenance of the status quo that has served them. They favor it even though supporting the status quo can set in stone the aspects of our society that have been and will continue to be unfair to people of color.

But group interest is not limited to whites. People of color are also likely to support ideas and actions that serve them and the people in their racial groups. One reason antiracism is so attractive to people of color is that it focuses so intensely on addressing their racialized struggles. So far, so good. But would not a person of color also have an interest in using antiracism to gain power that goes beyond the problems they face due to racism? In the rubric of antiracism, what measure do we have to make sure the justice sought by people of color is equal to the injustice they have suffered? Group interest theory would suggest that there is no natural limiting factor to how people of color may use newfound power against whites.

For example, look at the concept of white fragility championed by Robin DiAngelo (2018). If a person of color challenges a white person, she criticizes whites who "argue, minimize, explain, play devil's advocate, pout, tune out or withdraw to stop the challenge" (p. 112). So how are whites supposed to handle being critiqued by people of color? She states that whites should take that feedback and "graciously receive it, reflect and work to change the behavior" (p. 113). That may be good advice for all of us. But she offers no limit to how people of color treat whites in conversation. This sets up a situation where a person of color can be abusive in the use of power. In theory if a black coworker decides to verbally abuse a white coworker, the white worker should just take the abuse. What if a black male coworker makes inappropriate sexual comments to a white female coworker he coaches in a racialized framework? Can she complain? If she does, can the black coworker claim she is using a racialized stereotype against him? Within the rubric of DiAngelo's arguments, I fail to see how we are to stop the male coworker from engaging in sexualized verbal abuse. People of color are not any more likely to take advantage of an atmosphere where they gain power over others (and an atmosphere where people of color can complain about whites but the opposite is not allowed clearly represents power), but they are not any less likely to do so either. Group interest theory would predict that a philosophy of antiracism will lead to the misuse of power by people of color.

Some of the violence we have observed in protest rallies indicates the truth of that prediction. The vast majority of those who protested did so peacefully. I had friends and family members who went to protests, and all of them were ready to leave at the first sign of violence. But elsewhere, violence did occur. Some of it was sickening, such as the assault on Adam Haner, who was kicked in the head by a Black Lives Matter protester in Portland and lay unconscious in the street.

Perhaps even more troubling was the violence that occurred after the shooting of Ricardo Muñoz in Lancaster, Pennsylvania, when protesters smashed the windows of police cars and administrative buildings. But body camera footage showed Muñoz clearly charging the officers with a knife. It is hard to see what else the police could have done to protect themselves or others. The footage was produced almost immediately. Yet violence occurred anyway.

What happened here was not justice for someone who was killed while unarmed. Muñoz likely was mentally unbalanced and needed help. However, he presented a very real threat to the police and others when he wielded a large knife. There is a need for a discussion of how to change police procedures in a way that minimizes the need to put law enforcement officers in a situation where they must use violence. But once they are in the situation and being attacked, it is hard to fault them for not wanting to get stabbed. Yet activists did very little to seek out true justice. They had the power to create a riot and several of them used that power.

Antiracism is a potential solution for the many ways racism continues to manifest itself in our society. But it is a limited solution. As a solution it looks only to help people of color. There is little to no consideration of how it may lead people of color to engage in actions ranging from verbal abuse in a white fragility situation to violence even when police act in self-defense; it does not consider that there are other actors involved who deserve to be respected and protected. Antiracism cannot provide us with complete solutions to the problem of racial alienation. It generates efforts to help deal with racial injustice, but the way it does so does not consider how those efforts create their own types of unfairness.

BUT SHOULD NOT WHITES HAVE THE GREATER BURDEN?

One reaction to my complaints about antiracism is that whites should have a greater burden than people of color. This greater burden is not unfairness but justice. Given our history of racial abuse, it is not realistic to think people of color automatically do more work than whites because of the emotional burden they take on. Whites have gained more in our society because of this abuse, so they should have the greater responsibility in reconstructing a new egalitarian society. Since whites have been the major beneficiaries of our racial past, justice demands that they give more now in order for people of color to have equality.

I am not unsympathetic to this argument. I suspect that the solutions we arrive at as we work through the pain in our racialized society will result in unequal contributions by whites and nonwhites. Indeed, research on multiracial churches (Christerson, Edwards, & Emerson, 2005) indicates that church attendees of the numerical majority group have to make more cultural adjustments than the new racial group coming in. In this country whites have been the group with not only the numerical majority but also the dominant power in our society. It is realistic to think that ultimately they will have to make greater adjustments going forward than people of color.

But that does not mean people of color do not have to make any adjustments. Nor does it mean racial minorities get to obtain whatever they want in the process. Even calls for justice come with limits. Balance is needed between righting the wrongs in our society and being fair to whites. If we allowed an open-ended approach to justice, could African Americans not demand hundreds of years of white slavery to equal out the hundreds of years of black slavery? I do not blame whites for not wanting to totally submit to the desires of antiracist activists. They do not have the best interest of those whites at heart.

Here is a dynamic that occurs quite often. I will run into a white person who is quite serious about engaging with racism. They have become convinced that institutional and historical racial issues must be dealt with. They want to work at rebuilding dysfunctional race relations and listen to people of color. So they get involved in antiracism or a similar type of philosophy. But they are turned off by the expectation that their opinion does not matter because they are white. They know this is not the path to ending racial alienation but do not want to go back to a colorblind existence. Such a person now is left in frustration since it is clear that neither ignoring racial issues nor engaging in antiracism will get us where we need to go. Antiracism is inadequate for reaching whites who want to address racism but do not want to be relegated to passive "yes" men or women and be forced to ignore potential injustices perpetrated by antiracists.

To exemplify, let me tell you about Sally. Sally grew up in Mississippi and went to predominantly white schools. She was

curious about why her hometown was so segregated, with different racial groups worshiping separately. She had had cross-
cultural experiences that showed her the beauty and diversity
of God's people. One was attending a math and science school
her junior and senior years, where she met many students
whose parents were immigrants. Another was being involved
with a church plant in New York where members worked with
refugees. These experiences produced even more questions
about why blacks and whites went to separate institutions.

In her senior year at the University of Mississippi she took
an African American literature class. In this course she
learned about the history of racial integration at the university. Then on campus one weekend three white men in a
fraternity put a noose on the statue of James Meredith, the
first black to attend U of M. That day as one of the few white
students in her literature class, she listened to the black students talk about the racism they experienced and how some
whites might not welcome them given this racist incident.
Listening helped Sally develop empathy for black students.
This was also the same year as the death of Michael Brown.
Sally became more aware of the racial tension and conflict
emerging in society.

After she graduated Sally became involved in campus
ministry at the University of Mississippi. She would be with
the ministry for the next three years. The ministry was predominantly white, so she had conversations with those students on racial issues. This ministry focused on mission trips
and evangelism, and the students were interested in having
conservations across racial lines. But the ministry remained

monolithic, and Sally wondered why. Next she started discussion groups based on a Christian curriculum. The literature was based on antiracism principles, although Sally did not realize it at the time. Engaging students in the values found in that literature became part of her ministry.

Toward the end of her time as a college minister Donald Trump was elected president. At the time she learned from the group behind her antiracism literature the argument that the United States is inherently racist. The election of Trump seemed like powerful evidence of this reality, particularly the attitudes of individuals on Facebook who supported the way Trump discussed issues such as refugees, immigration, and race. The rhetoric seemed to reinforce the accuracy of the antiracist critique of the United States as fundamentally racist. Sally rejected critiques from other Christians that went against her ideals of social justice and antiracism.

However, she began to see an inability of others to ask questions within the antiracism circles she was involved in at her church and the antiracist Facebook group she participated in. She saw a disturbing tone when questions were raised. Whites who asked questions could be labeled as racist or fragile. Questions that came from people of color led to accusations of internalized racism. Informal rules in the Facebook group, such as people not being able to challenge any assertions by people of color, forestalled debate. Sally concluded that instead of reconciling with each other, individuals were being reconciled to an ideology.

But Sally had questions she wanted to ask. One example was about police shootings. She had seen a video of an unarmed white man being shot even though he was following police commands. Her previous understanding was that such unarmed shootings happened only to black men. She wanted to ask questions to make sense of this but knew she was not allowed to do that. Conversation was not welcome if it involved disagreement with people of color by whites. Sally saw this dynamic in other parts of the country as well.

In the antiracism Facebook group she saw one man willing to ask some of the same questions she had even though he met resistance. He was asking questions such as the importance of truth regardless of the ethnicity of the speaker. Sally was interested in his analysis of critical race theory. Reading his comments and online articles helped her realize that reality was more nuanced than the oppressor-oppressed dichotomy she was being fed in her antiracism groups. The turning point was a story about a black church being burned down that had then been defaced with the word *Trump* painted on it. She was outraged and saw the incident as evidence of the story antiracism had taught her. She assumed the crime had been committed by a white supremacist. She later found out that a black member of the church had committed the crime with the intent of making it seem politically motivated. This helped her realize that reality differed from her antiracism interpretation.

It was never enough for Sally to just proclaim the gospel. Her beliefs had important ethical implications, and she believed God wanted justice. But pursuing justice also meant pursuing the truth. Her antiracism framework for interpreting events was missing important pieces. Aspects of this ideology were helpful in aiding her understanding of what had happened in our nation, but if this was the only framework one used, then it was incomplete. She sought friends who allowed for broader discussion on racial issues and became open to criticism of social justice. She believed that while we might have different ideas about what justice is, truth does not depend on who teaches it. Truth is independent of its source, whether a black woman or a white man. These incongruencies eventually made antiracism incompatible with her theological beliefs.

Sally does not feel called to walk away from her concerns about racial inequality and wants to write about these issues. But she sees the reduction of everything to power and race in antiracism as unhealthy to individuals and incompatible with her faith. She has taken a more balanced approach compared to the totalizing view of antiracism but also understands that racial partiality still exists. She warns others not to fall into a false dichotomy that one must be all in for antiracism or else one is either a racist or does not care about justice at all.

Sally is an example of a white person who wants to become an ally to people of color but cannot under the terms of antiracism. Those terms are not inclusive enough for Sally and do not allow her the intellectual freedom she craves. A movement to deal with racial animosity must have support from as many people as possible and we cannot unnecessarily alienate people like Sally. We cannot simply say whites have the greater burden without also recognizing the responsibilities we people of color have to humanize potential white allies and address their concerns.

Some will state that if these whites are not willing to get with the program, we can just leave them behind. They will argue that we must have justice before we have unity. Actually, it is the other way around. We need unity before we can get justice. People of color should demand that they have their voice heard, but we do not have to demand that others shut up. We can learn from the perspectives of others as we build a unified coalition for justice that includes all of us. If we want justice, we have to do the hard work of building unity in a respectful manner. Only then can we as a society implement solutions that will not be sabotaged by the large percentage of the country that feels they had no say in how those solutions were constructed.

CONCLUSION

I do not see how antiracist approaches can produce sustainable solutions. Activists tend to apply cultural pressure on society to comply with the solutions they have chosen. I understand why they take such an approach. Those of us of color have suffered from centuries of racial abuse. We have been silenced in a racialized society that disregards us. We have been held back and not allowed to live out our full potential. Under such conditions, a desire for mandatory lessons for whites and rules that favor us is completely understandable. There is an emotional satisfaction to be found in finally getting our turn at cultural power. But ultimately this approach does not work. It is not effective in producing social changes and it gains allies largely due to compulsion rather than conviction. It relies on power rather than moral suasion, and while there are times when we need to use power, it is much better to get what we want through moral suasion.

The element of antiracism that requires whites to take a passive, supportive role is problematic. Efforts to relegate whites to such a place in our racial conversations are destined to energize resistance. Most if not all of the negative elements of antiracism emerge from attempts to decenter the perspectives of whites. Some will argue that I am presenting an unfair definition of antiracism by highlighting this concept. But in all the antiracism literature I have read, this devaluing is either implied or strongly advocated. If there are any antiracism works that welcome the perspectives of whites in an honest dialogue, I would welcome the opportunity to read them. But even then, such literature would be an exception to the general trend among antiracists to denigrate everything connected to whiteness. The seeds of improving antiracism can be planted in efforts to include whites as equal—not superior or inferior—partners in the discussion of how we end multifaceted racism.

The big question is how we deal fairly with our history of racial abuse. How do we make certain we are being fair to the people of color who have suffered from that racial abuse? How do we make certain that in our efforts to do justice we do not create injustice in the other direction? It is fair to say that colorblindness does not show enough concern for correcting the wrongs done to people of color and antiracism does not show enough concern for the possibility of overcorrection. However, a more balanced path can lead us away from both extremes and toward a sustainable solution that levels these competing interests. The mutual accountability model is philosophically sound, and empirical evidence shows it can succeed where colorblindness and antiracism have failed.

THE EMPIRICAL BASIS OF MUTUAL ACCOUNTABILITY

I HAVE CRITICIZED both colorblindness and antiracism for lacking empirical support. Neither approach comports with an accurate assessment of social reality. Both bring certain presuppositions into the discussion of how we deal with racial alienation, and those presuppositions are not empirically supported. But if I am going to complain about a lack of empirical evidence for colorblindness or antiracism, then I had better be ready to present empirical evidence supporting mutual accountability. Fortunately, there is evidence supporting this model. After looking at scholarly theories about why it will work, I will more explicitly discuss that evidence.

THE CONTACT HYPOTHESIS

One of the most important theories for helping us understand barriers to healthy relationships is the contact hypothesis. The contact hypothesis is relatively simple. It asserts that the more contact we have with people in a given group, the more likely we are to become tolerant of them and the less likely we are to be negatively biased toward them. But while the contact hypothesis seems simple at first, it soon becomes clear that we cannot just bring a bunch of people together and wait for them to become friends. Early research (Cohen, 1984; Deutsch & Collins, 1951; St. John, 1975) indicates that interracial contact in educational and residential settings does not necessarily lead to better race relations. For the contact to have a positive effect, it must occur under the right conditions. Other empirical research (Pettigrew & Tropp, 2006; Yancey, 2007) suggests that under those conditions, intergroup contact produces more tolerance and less prejudice. Generally, productive contact is between individuals who have equal status, are noncompetitive, have a close relationship, and are supported by relevant authority figures. When contact occurs under these conditions, we are more likely to have better race relations. Needless to say, interracial contact in an atmosphere of hostility is not likely to decrease racial alienation.

Even though I am black, I was not focused on racial issues during the early part of my life. Until I lost my first girlfriend, I really did not think deeply about racism. I had seen it in my life and the lives of others, but I generally focused on other matters. After that experience I wanted to find ways to deal with racism. I did not want to go through that rejection again or have anyone else do so. When I started to conduct research on racial issues, it was not enough for me to document the problems of racism. I wanted to find solutions, especially solutions others may have overlooked. This eventually led me to research the potential power of interracial contact. I wound up doing a good deal of work investigating religious institutions and marriages, two areas where the conditions of positive interracial contact can be met.

Based on my research I found that interracial contact, done correctly, is vital for producing positive racial change in our society. I found evidence that in the right circumstances interracial contact helps whites be more sensitive to the plight of people of color (Yancey, 1999, 2007). It also helps people of color learn to navigate the larger society and may contribute to their economic success (Yancey, 2007). It is not a panacea, and if done incorrectly, interracial contact can make things worse. But my work has convinced me that we will not adequately deal with racial alienation until we have interacted with each other in healthier ways.

This is not a "let us all be friends and racism will go away" argument. Our history of racial abuse mandates that at some level we have to make serious structural changes in our society. But the research on interracial contact indicates that to make those changes in ways that benefit the most individuals in our society, we have to enjoy healthier interracial relationships. Although not the entire solution, those relationships are a necessary factor in combating racial alienation.

AN OVERARCHING IDENTITY

Another important factor in dealing with racial strife is social identity. Research shows that our social identity helps us establish who we accept as members of our ingroup and who we reject as members of our outgroup. It is the interaction of

individuals who perceive each other as members of outgroups that leads to racial tension. One reason interracial
contact may matter is that it helps us identify with people we
normally think of as part of our outgroup. Research indicates
that when we share an overarching identity with those with
whom we are in contact, we move from seeing them as for-
eigners to seeing them as part of our group (Gaertner,
Dovidio, & Bachman, 1996). At that point our biases toward
former outgroup members tend to drop dramatically. An
integral part of how we lessen racial tension is to stop thinking
of ourselves as "them" and "us." We need to be thinking of
all of us as "us."

When I was an undergraduate student, I had strong loyalty
to my dorm. In part this may have been because I was a res-
ident assistant and worked for the dorm, but it also tended to
be where I developed my friendships. My dormmates and I
ate together, played intermural sports together, and hung out
in the dorm lobby together. We generally competed against
the other male dorms and saw them as our enemies. It felt
great when we beat them in intermural sports or other com-
petitions. We had our own set of stereotypes for the "losers"
in other dorms. Funny how easy it was to create members of
an outgroup simply by living in a different dorm.

But this outgrouping ended when we attended sporting
events for the college. Then we all cheered for our school and
dorm loyalties went out the window. The animosity between
us lifted for a few hours, because for those few hours we had
an overarching identity with our college that transcended our
dorm identity. Likewise, the more we develop an overarching

identity with others in our society, the less hostility we will have with each other. We can use that identity to focus more on what we have in common than on what divides us.

There is a natural limitation embedded in my example. When I felt closer to those in my college who lived in different dorms during a sporting event, I felt further away from those in the other college. This often happens when we look to develop an overarching identity. In fact, one of the easiest ways to develop an overarching identity is to find a common enemy we can unite against. We saw this after 9/11. There was a unity in our society we had rarely seen before, but that unity came at the expense of Muslims who experienced increased Islamophobia. Is it possible for us to create an overarching identity without scapegoating another group?

It is possible to do this, but it will be very difficult. We will have to be inclusive in ways that so far have escaped us. We cannot impose the demands of our group on others. Negotiate for those demands, yes. Impose them, no. Efforts to force others to accept our ideas will create resentment and make it harder to establish unity. Rather than trying to make sure our group wins everything it can get, we must seek common ground and do our best for all to win. The process of communicating and negotiating with others can be frustrating, but if done properly it can also bring us together. It can create community. If we can overcome our tendencies to get everything we want and insist we are right and instead learn to fashion win-win solutions, we have a chance to move forward.

This is what collaborative conversation is about. It is about learning to work together to find solutions most of us can accept. It is developing a connection with others by building an overarching identity where it is not us versus them but just us working together. It is learning we cannot get everything. Indeed, any group that gets everything will sow seeds of resistance among other groups. This means the winning group must either find ways to oppress and take away the rights of those who resist or watch that resistance sabotage their efforts. Collaborative conversation means differentiating what we need from what we want in our demands so we can give up the latter to receive support for the former. If we want to develop an overarching identity to help lessen our racial tension—and this is what research suggests we should do—then a model of conversation instead of compulsion is what we need. Theories about contact, identity, and intergroup relations favor a mutual accountability approach.

RESEARCH SUPPORTING COLLABORATION

While it is important to look at theories about why mutual accountability may work, it is also vital to examine research showing potential fruits of this approach. In other words, what do empirical efforts say about how attempts to foster productive communication ameliorate racial tension? All the theories in the world will not help us unless we have real results.

To date there is no research on how a collaborative conversation approach may affect racial bias or prejudice. However, this style of communication has been shown to be effective in producing goal-oriented beneficial outcomes (Fausel, 1998; MacPherson, 2010) and creating an atmosphere of volitional compliance (Mohr, Fisher, & Nevin, 1996). Volitional compliance offers a potentially better path toward attitude alteration than a teacher-student approach in which an expert imparts his or her perspective on others. Other work indicates that families with a collaborative orientation have more positive interactions and relations with each other (Ellis & Fisher, 1994). Learning to work together within families can produce a common identity that creates a more positive atmosphere for members of those families. Having members of racial outgroups learn to work together can enhance an atmosphere that reduces intergroup tensions.

Research indicates that to engage in moral suasion we generally need to identify agreement with others, admit when others are right, build rapport, and accurately understand the ideas of others (Cialdini, 2001; Paulus, 2006; Watkins, 2001). All these elements are important components of collaborative conversation. To the degree that we utilize moral suasion to gain allies or promote certain ideas, it is much more effective to engage in the techniques of collaborative conversation than to attempt to use power to force compliance. We can get individuals to comply, but they are unlikely to change deeply held beliefs. Such allies can quickly be lost when the wind of what is socially acceptable changes.

Some may fear relying on moral suasion because it seems to take the power of change out of our hands. Instead, it is in the hands of others to decide whether they are persuaded to take a course we want them to take. There is a temptation to spoon-feed others the ideas we want them to have and prevent them from considering alternative approaches. It is true that if people are surrounded only by "approved" opinions, they are more likely to accept those opinions. But that commitment will be shallow. These individuals will not have thought through their ideas carefully but will instead seek only the right marching orders. Research shows that when people are not exposed to different opinions, they become less willing to consider alternate views as legitimate and become overconfident they are right (Sunstein & Hastie, 2015). They develop the type of overconfidence that can lead to witch hunts for ideological dissenters and a need to ignore evidence that contradicts their beliefs.

If we want individuals who are able to engage in nuanced intellectual discourse, then we cannot hide dissenting opinions. When individuals encounter dissenting opinions through diversified social networks, they may change their original beliefs. Research has shown that when people have a variety of ideological influences in their lives, they tend to at least moderate their beliefs (Kim, 2015; Mutz, 2006). If they keep their original ideas, they will be better thinkers and more nuanced (Butnor, 2012; Hong & Page, 2004; Mannix & Neale, 2005). They will not only have belief but the ability to articulate those beliefs in their own words. Moral suasion to bring someone to a particular perspective will create superior long-term results relative to using power to lead them into accepting an ideology. If short-term results are more important to us than long-term changes, then by all means seek to use political, cultural, or social power. If you can keep the shaming and political pressure on, you can compel support, but you do so at the cost of creating shallow "believers."

There is a philosophical and even moral dimension to the question of using coercion to convince others. If individuals are not morally persuaded to support or at least accept certain ideas, then one will have to use coercive measures to gain and maintain support. Those measures may be informal, such as expressing disappointment at disagreeing opinions, but it rarely stops there. Once we have unleashed the potential to punish ideological opponents, this potential is not easily contained. It easily escalates from expression of disagreement to employment termination (Fisher, 2020; Geran Pilon, 2020) and institutional silencing of speakers (Jackson, 2016). It quickly becomes about power and using that power against ideological enemies. Is this the culture we want to live in? Do we want to live in fear that if we state the wrong comment, we will be punished?

If not, the only path out of an arms race of cultural punishment is to move away from a warlike mentality in how we address issues of racial alienation. Collaboration and cooperation must replace stigma and punishment for us to avoid this fate. We all should deliberately think about which path we want to tread. This choice is a choice concerning our values, and empirical work cannot help us make that choice. But if we select collaboration and cooperation, research can help us figure out the best way to achieve that goal.

COLLABORATIVE COMMUNICATION AND STRUCTURAL CHANGE

What about collaborative communication and healthy interracial communication when it comes to making institutional or structural changes? Are such attempts at communication merely ways to maintain the status quo? Can focusing on healthy interracial communication really result in alterations in how we run our organizations and formulate our laws? I believe that the win-win attitude we find in collaborative communication is important in finding solutions that will change our social structures and institutions. Not only will such an approach help us find solutions, it will help those solutions be sustainable as they gain support across racial and political dimensions. We know that collaborative styles of communication lead to less prejudice and more volitional compliance in the decisions that are made (Ellis & Fisher, 1994). Not only might we find better solutions by working together, we are also more likely to have solutions that are supported by a strong majority of those who participated in crafting those structural and institutional changes.

To look at how this happens let us go back to the research I noted in the last chapter (Dobbin & Kalev, 2016) about the failure of companies to hire more managers of color. We found that mandatory diversity training, implementing job tests as a requirement for new managers,[1] and a grievance system for people of color correlated with fewer managers of color. That was the bad news. However, the researchers also examined companies that tried to increase the number of managers of color with voluntary diversity training and by using mostly white managers to recruit people of color out of college, to mentor people of color, and to head up diversity task forces. They found that five years later there were significantly more managers of color at these companies. What is the difference between the tools that work and those that do not? I suggest that the methods that do not work tend to be geared at forcing whites to "do the right thing." We can see this in the compulsion to force white managers to attend diversity training and use job tests to screen out applicants. Grievance systems also can be seen as a way to place an institutional check on white managers. Such systems may be used as a threat to make certain whites conduct themselves in ways that are deemed sufficiently racially aware. The desire to make certain that the whites who potentially hire people of color have institutional checks that work to our advantage is understandable. Given our history of racial abuse and research indicating that there still is racial bias in hiring (Quillian et al., 2017), people of color and antiracists generally welcome such checks. The problem is that instead of obtaining the desired result of more managers of color, we end up with fewer managers of color.

But the measures that lead to more managers of color tend to be more focused on bringing whites into the conversation rather than compelling them to do right by people of color. If a company has a mostly, or even all, white managerial team and wants to become more racially diverse, then making training voluntary and using those white managers to plan how to become more diverse and to mentor the new hires of color are ways to bring those white managers into the conversation about how the company can become more diverse. Bringing European Americans into the conversation of increasing diversity is more effective at getting people of color hired than keeping whites out of the conversation or forcing them to capitulate to preordained notions of antiracism. We should do what works and including whites in the conversation is empirically superior than keeping them out of that conversation.

Introducing whites into the larger discussion of how to become more racially diverse is deeply reflective of a mutual accountability approach. This represents a multiracial effort to work together to find lasting solutions. White managers who are successful likely gain input from people of color, but they themselves are not silenced with charges of fragility or privilege. Working together to find solutions that serve everyone, the white managers currently in the company and the people of color who will be brought in as new hires, is a core idea within mutual accountability.

LESSONS FROM DIVERSITY PROGRAMS

Diversity programs often do not succeed. But we can still learn from them. A meta-analysis (Bezrukova, Spell, Perry, & Jehn, 2016) provides important information about developing awareness as a value for diversity programs. This work found that the smallest effects came from merely teaching individuals about their attitudes and behaviors. The most effective programs were the ones that combined awareness with the development of skills that allow the individual to be better situated to deal with a multicultural atmosphere. Another meta-analysis indicates that intergroup contact and cooperative interventions within diversity training efforts have promising potential to reduce prejudice (Paluck & Green, 2009). It is not enough to teach people what to think; we also must walk beside them to develop the proper skills. Research is making it clear that a diversity model where people sit and listen to a diversity expert, even a highly skilled diversity expert, is one of the least effective models one can use. Rather, developing skills that aid in cooperation in a multicultural atmosphere offers the best chance at success. Active listening and learning how to communicate with others are skills that need to increase.

An online article (Baron, 2019) points out that people generally do not identify as racist. Those who want to convince them otherwise have a high hill to climb. I remember being a teaching assistant in an introductory sociology course. I sat in the back of the class to take notes for the professor. I looked about the same age as the students and I blended in so well that the students soon forget who I was. When the topic of race came up, the professor talked about white supremacy and the KKK. The students were unmoved. In fact, I saw a great deal of eye rolling. Overt expression of racism was totally foreign in the lives of my students. They did not relate to it. I understand that the professor was trying to motivate them into caring about racism, but trying to make them feel guilty about racism is not the right approach. Baron points out that empowerment, not coercion, is key to creating real change. Indicating that mandatory training is not as effective as voluntary training, she notes that coercion is a barrier to producing a welcoming environment to people of color. If we provide majority and minority group members with tools to create a welcoming environment, we will have a better situation than what we gain by using social pressure to create a better atmosphere.

Furthermore, taking the perspective of others has been shown to enhance the effectiveness of diversity training programs (Lindsey et al., 2015). When we encourage others to consider the perspective of others, they can appreciate diversity in a low-pressure atmosphere. This helps us reduce the possibility of backlash, which research has documented is quite possible when individuals see diversity training as punishment or as a reaction to the shortcomings of those undergoing the training (Sanchez & Medkik, 2004). Perspective taking is more likely with interracial contact if that contact allows for honest conversations and individuals intentionally attempt to take the perspectives of others. It stands to reason that one of the skills that needs to be developed through diversity training is learning to understand the perspective of individuals of other races. Teaching individuals how to engage in active listening and to accurately communicate their perspectives to others is key to mutual accountability, and research indicates that learning these skills is one of the best outcomes of any diversity program.

While diversity programs for the most part have been unsuccessful in producing useful outcomes, looking at when they are successful informs us about the direction we need to go if we want to address racial alienation. We need less focus on teaching individuals about other cultures and more focus on developing skills that aid in living in a multicultural society. We need to focus less on "forcing" individuals into diversity programs and more on showing them the value of developing skills offered by the programs. Since perspective taking is a valuable skill for individuals to learn, we need to teach individuals how to understand and learn about the perspectives of cultural or racial others. Finally, we must avoid thinking that this is an easy one-time process. To provide training that is valuable, it is important to make a long-term commitment to the process. Not all diversity programs are the same. Those that include collaborative factors are more likely to succeed, and if we want diversity programs to be worth the money, then we should look at including those elements.

COLLABORATIVE COMMUNICATION
IN THE LIFE OF MONIQUE

Sometimes it is useful to take a step back from the evidence and just look at the power of positive interracial contact and collaborative communication in the life of a single person. Chantal "Monique" Duson grew up in South Central Los Angeles. Despite growing up in that predominantly black neighborhood, she did not have much of a race consciousness until as a young teenager she saw the riots associated with Rodney King's beating. Many of the events associated with the riots, such as the beating of Reginald Denny, occurred only a few blocks from her. The conversations around the riots helped her hear the complaints of blacks and become more aware of her own blackness. Furthermore, her teachers in fifth and sixth grade also taught her to have pride in her blackness. Monique did not have a lot of white friends growing up in South Central LA. However, at age fifteen she moved to North Hollywood, where she experienced more exposure to whites. Some of her interaction with whites reinforced her mistrust of them. For example, she observed white women clutching their purses when coming close to her. Such actions substantiated her negative feelings toward whites she had developed through conversations with other blacks.

In college she took sociology courses that increased her awareness of racism and encouraged her to further educate herself about the racial problems in our society. These teachings automatically flowed into the train of thought she had previously developed. She accepted the ideas in those courses without questioning them because they fit so well with her experience. Those ideas taught her that she was different from whites and whites would not understand her. At college she helped to head up the multiethnic and black student group. This group wanted to make people aware of the issues facing students of color and the need for justice.

After college Monique started to work in group homes and case management. She used her job to elevate junior high and high school students of color so they were equipped to face systemic racism. She sought to remind them of their challenges and said they would have to work hard to overcome racial barriers. Her work allowed her to express her activism. She later became a missionary to South Africa for four years. That trip provided more evidence for the racism of whites. She saw the disdain white South Africans had toward blacks; sometimes she was even pushed by white women. The black Africans talked about their support of socialism as well as wanting to combat white oppression and racism. Monique found herself in agreement.

After returning to the United States she moved in with a white roommate. The two women began to have deep conservations on race. She also got to know a white intern in her work, who talked about how students of color were demeaning white students at her college and how white teachers were being fired. The intern related experiences of white students being yelled at in class. Monique began to investigate and found that much of what had been said was true. Her interactions with these two women began to allow Monique to start questioning her previous beliefs. She wondered if those beliefs could be creating this animosity. She wondered why whites did not see injustice, but she also questioned what was happening to create such strife. She did not want whites to suffer the way her intern was suffering. She began to think that a wrong cannot be corrected with another wrong.

Monique realized that the thought of whites being her sisters and brothers was not as deeply ingrained as she had previously believed. She had more of an "us and them" view rather than being united with others. She also realized that her ethnicity was more important than her faith. These realizations led her to begin questioning the way terms like *justice* were used. But she also began to see through her faith that there were specific ways we should see what is right and what is wrong. Using the concept of injustice for anything we disagree with expands the term beyond any reasonable use.

Today Monique believes that Christians can and should seek to change biblically unjust laws and systems. However, what we should consider first is whether we are acting justly with those we have influence over and within our own communities. Look for businesses that are not upholding justice and doing what is right. Engage with those who exhibit racism on a personal level. We can use our voice, vote, and dollar to create change. She believes that institutional racism is real but it may not be as all-encompassing as some people make it out to be. She does not accept the notion that all of America is racist. She believes that we may find racism in the police force, but that does not make all police racist. While institutional racism may be real, it is also poorly defined. On the other hand, she argues that colorblindness is unrealistic. We cannot just ignore race because of our own personal weaknesses. She believes that ethnic partiality and hatred create racism, and since race is socially constructed, people can be tempted to use those constructions to create inequalities. Furthermore, doing away with race eliminates the beauty of culture. As a result of her new direction on these issues, she has started the Center for Biblical Unity (see centerforbiblicalunity.com), which provides resources and training to help individuals explore their own biases.

Monique traveled the journey of mistrust of whites to sympathy for those being mistreated. That journey tore her from a path of seeking solutions for "her people" to working for solutions that benefit everyone. Her relative lack of contact with whites early in her life led to the sort of stereotyping and misunderstandings that feed racial alienation. She is now in a position where she is working to bridge the racial divide, whereas before her actions and suspicions toward whites served to widen that divide. Her interactions with whites and deep productive conversations were important catalysts for this transformation. Research suggests that efforts to produce more collaborative conversations and to build a common social identity will have similar effects on others. But it is not just talk. Monique's desire to make change is organizational as well as personal. And as we will soon see, collaborative conversation can and should be part of generating the results we want.

WHAT ABOUT IGNORING RACIAL ISSUES?

Since I have focused more on comparing mutual accountability to other proactive efforts, let me offer a quick word about a colorblind approach. Despite beliefs to the contrary, people of color still face barriers due to their race. We saw in chapter two that historical racism continues to impact racial minorities. This reality obviously creates pain for nonwhites. Denial of pain has not been proven to be a good way to handle it (Cooper-White, 2012; Miller, 2002; Wolfelt, 2004). Efforts of those espousing colorblindness are unlikely to help the victims of racism have confidence that they can fully participate in our society. We cannot ignore the wounds of people of color and hope that time will heal those wounds. Time does not heal wounds. Effort and commitment are what is needed to heal wounds.

Our racial history has led us to our current situation. To figure out how to mitigate the damage done by this history, we can look at academic research on whether our previous efforts have been successful. That research (Blum, 2002; Bonilla-Silva, 2006; Gallagher, 2003; Neville, Gallardo, & Sue, 2016; Yi, Todd, & Mekawi, 2020) indicates that ignoring the continuing effects of racism will not be effective. Our empirical evidence indicates that relying on healthy interracial

contact and mutually committing to enter productive interracial conversations where we can find solutions with which
everyone can live are most effective. The mutual accountability model is about directly addressing the racial pain in
our society in an atmosphere of cooperation and care. That
care offers us the best chance of healing the wounds in a
racialized society.

CONCLUSION

The evidence to date indicates that a process like mutual accountability offers the best approach for dealing with racial
tension. Helping others engage in perspective taking and
promoting healthy interracial contact are empirically supported as ways to improve intergroup relations. To date there
has not been a good deal of direct research on the use of
collaborative conversations in specifically racialized situations, but other research of this approach in other arenas
does not raise any notable shortcomings of this approach and
a lot of upside. In time I hope to see more research testing
the use of collaborative conversations on race relations, but
with the sort of promise empirical evidence has delivered
thus far, those conversations are the best direction for us.
Since we have a viable alternative supported by empirical research, we have reason to get out of the rut of either ignoring
racial issues or using antiracist strategies that have not shown
signs of success.

THE THEOLOGICAL
BASIS OF MUTUAL
ACCOUNTABILITY

AFTER THE PASSAGE OF RESOLUTION NINE in the 2019
Southern Baptist Convention, several voices rose to condemn
it. The resolution argued that issues of critical race theory and
intersectionality should not be used as competing worldviews
to Christianity, but they could be used as tools for social
analysis. Arguments against the resolution included that it was
designed to make all whites feel guilty (Maples, 2019; Peacock,
2020) and pushed notions of institutional racism (Ascol, 2020;
Manning, 2020). These arguments were a repackaging of
many of the ideas of colorblindness. There is a sense among
critics of resolution nine that critical race theory and intersectionality are efforts to provide special assistance to people of
color. Efforts to root out and deal with institutional discrimination are dismissed out of hand by such critics.

I could argue that the critics' position is unreasonable. By
dismissing the insights gained from a fair analysis of the
impact of our social structures, they remain blind to unfair

pressures experienced by people of color. The callousness with which they treat the pain of racial minorities when they run into these institutional barriers has driven many people of color from evangelicalism. But that is not what bothered me most. What bothered me most was their repackaging of our Christian faith in a colorblind framework. When we take part in this repackaging, we imply that our Christian faith does not have anything new to offer the discussion. That our faith can only contextualize ideas developed in a secular framework. The critics took the values of their dominant white culture and imposed it on the rest of the Bible.

Yes, this repackaging also occurs among Christians seeking to implement antiracism measures. It is disheartening for the same reasons as the repackaging within a colorblind framework. Racism, and the intergroup conflict that arises from it, is one of the great moral issues of our day. Does not our faith have something unique and special to offer? Can we not go beyond our cultural norms to deal with this moral issue? Or are we relegated simply to parroting what we hear from the larger society and repackaging it in a Christian voice?

When I decided to tackle issues of racism, I decided that if my Christian path was the path to moral truth, then it must offer more than what we gain from the rest of society. As Christians we are called to be obedient to the Bible and our faith. In theory this calls us to place biblical truth above all other efforts to gain knowledge. This requirement has become a source of contention in our society. Those who are not Christians often think it unwise to rely so much on the Bible for wisdom. Even some Christians question the wisdom of looking to the Bible in such an exclusive manner (Yancey & Quosigk, 2021). This often is expressed in the idea that religion and science are in competition. I reject that assertion.

I am both a Christian and social scientist. I have found that good theology and good science generally go together; they are not in competition with each other. When they seem to contradict, what I have generally found is that there is either bad science or bad theology involved—sometimes both. Ironically, I think both bad science and bad theology come from the same source—a desire to make reality what we want it to be rather than what it is. When bad science and bad Christian theology told us blacks were inferior, it was because the whites of that day wanted to justify their cruelty to people like me. There is no contradiction between science and my faith. Truth is truth and we should look for it wherever we can find it. The search is consistent in both science and theology, because while some elements of truth are indisputable in both science and theology, we also fall short of complete knowledge. A wise person recognizes that learning about reality will be a lifelong journey and beyond.

In the last chapter I showed that the mutual accountability model comports with scientific research. For many that is sufficient information to decide about the viability of this approach. But not for everyone. Many Christians want to know that this approach is grounded in their theological beliefs. Not only is this approach well-established in Christian theology, it is dictated by the implications of Christian theology. Indeed, it is my Christian beliefs and understanding of the contrast of those beliefs against a secular approach that inspired me to explore this option. If that type of theological thought is not of interest to you, feel free to skip this chapter; I believe the rest of the book can give you what you need to know about the utility and value of a mutual accountability perspective. But if you want to see my argument that a mutual accountability model is not merely a Christian approach to racial issues but rather should be *the* Christian approach to our racialized society, I encourage you to finish this chapter.

THE BIBLE ON RACE

Before I get into a Christian solution to racial issues, let me first address the idea of racism in the Bible. Simply put, the concept of race did not exist at the time when the Bible was written. Scholars generally argue that the idea of race developed in reaction to the trans-Atlantic slave trade and was used to justify the transformation of blacks from indentured servants into chattel slaves (Buckwalter & Roberts, 2016; Winnubst, 2020). From that point whites developed ideas about white superiority and applied those ideas to nonwhites. If you went back into biblical times and talked about individuals as whites, blacks, or Hispanics, you would likely receive a confused look. God knew the concept of race would eventually develop, but it made no sense to discuss it in the Bible since it was an unknown concept at that time.

However, the Bible does talk about dealing with conflict between groups that do not like each other. Intergroup conflict is an ingrained part of human history and of course the Bible discusses it.[1] For example, we know that Jews generally hated Samaritans. Samaritans were Jews who mixed with Assyrians and were considered "half-breeds." The Samaritans were the ones who harassed Nehemiah as he worked to rebuild the walls of Jerusalem (Nehemiah 6:1-14). They built their own temple in competition with the Jews. Samaria often shielded Jewish criminals (Joshua 20:6-7). All of this made the Jews hate them. They had no use for those they considered second-class citizens. Stories of the Good Samaritan and the Samaritan woman at the well are relevant for understanding an approach to intergroup conflict. Given the role of intergroup conflict in racial alienation, this is not a bad place to start as we consider a biblical approach to race.

What do these stories teach us about intergroup conflict? I am struck by how Jesus emphasizes the humanity of the Samaritans in both stories. He did so in a social world that did not consider Samaritans fully human, a world where Jews did not want Samaritans to have full human rights. The perspectives of Samaritans did not matter to Jews at that time. But Jesus showed that Samaritans could be heroes, as he did in the story of the Good Samaritan. He showed that they deserved to be treated with respect and to be listened to as he did with the woman at the well. Jesus did not exclude Samaritans. He went through Samaria when others avoided it. He deliberately used a Samaritan character in a positive manner in his parable. These choices were not lost on his disciples. Jesus was saying that these people have worth and must be included. No matter who engages us in conflict, we cannot forget that they are people of tremendous worth and should be treated that way.

This powerful notion is often lost on us because we have no emotional connection to Samaritans. But if we think about groups we do not like for political, religious, racial, or social reasons—or some combination of those reasons—we can begin to relate to what Jesus was telling the Jews. It is easy to talk about loving our enemies in the abstract, but it can be quite a bit harder to accept this when it comes to real people. Think of the group you hate the most. If you are a cultural conservative, you might consider abortion providers or sexual minority activists. If you are a cultural progressive, you might consider proselytizing street preachers or Proud Boys.

Those people are the Samaritans in your life. They are just as human as you are. They can be heroes and need to be treated with the respect you would demand for yourself. The message Jesus would have for you is to truly love those your subculture tells you to hate. Could you tell a story in which a person from that hated subculture was the hero? Jesus did. Could you go out of your way to treat that person with respect? Jesus did.

But treating others with respect and seeing them as human is not exactly a message unique to Christianity. Enlightenment thinkers argued that humans were rational and could move toward perfectibility. Modern humanism has built on enlightenment ideas to work toward systems that help humans maximize their full potential. There is an assumption that if we are given the proper environment and educational training, our rational and moral capacities will grow. With this growth we will fashion a better and happier society. Traditional societies based on tribalism and bigotry are barriers that will be overturned by institutions of science and education. Humans have great worth in the eyes of such thinkers and their greatness is being restrained by backward thinking. In one of my earlier studies (Yancey & Williamson, 2012), I investigated the ideas of cultural progressives, who tend to adopt these tenets of humanism. We found that because of their confidence in the intellectual and moral capacities of humanity, modern-day humanists assert that humans will flourish—all we have to do is remove the barriers of tribal religion. In their perspective, human potential is nearly limitless if we can get beyond the boundaries of religious fatalism.

The notion that humans are of great value is also true in the Christian tradition, although for different reasons. Humanists see us having value due to our higher evolutionary state and their idea that as rational creatures our choices must be respected. Christians see us having value due to the fact that we are children of the living God. God has created us, and being products in the hands of the Creator imputes tremendous value to us. How we maximize our value is different from humanism in that we concentrate on drawing closer to God rather than relying on our own rational capacities. But it is hard to argue that secular humanists value humans less than Christians. If we are looking for what Christians can uniquely add to the conversation, we will have to go beyond the idea that we all have great value. To find that type of distinction we look to a major difference between Christianity and secular ideologies—the concept of human depravity.

HUMAN DEPRAVITY VERSUS HUMAN PERFECTIBILITY

When we think about how Christian beliefs differ from secular ideologies, we usually focus on obvious differences, such as belief in the importance of the supernatural. But a more basic distinction often overlooked in this analysis is the nature of humans. Most secular ideologies promote the idea of human perfectibility. This is the idea that eventually we can create a better society through human effort and rationality. We can see this in many different forms of secular ideology. Marxists believe that once we reform our economic system, we will experience a Marxian utopia. Secular feminists contend that once we correct immoral gender roles and values, we will be able to overcome the patriarchal nature of our society. In secular libertarianism, the idea of human perfectibility comes from maximizing freedom from laws and regulations. Rationality, reason, and science are believed to be able to guide us to a better world.

How we think about the nature of humans has enormous implications for the sort of vision we have for society. If we trust humans to use their rational abilities to construct the best society for us, it makes sense to create a society that maximizes the abilities of individuals to contribute to our society. Our values come from our ability to use logic and reason to figure out the best values. We are better off using a trial-and-error approach until we can rationally deduce the best set of values for our society. But if our vision of humans is tied to notions of human depravity, then we are not so eager to rely on human abilities to establish societal values. Christians look for external sources of values through our monotheistic faith.

Even if one does not believe in a Christian God but still accepts notions of human depravity, it remains important to find ways to control for that depravity. If our vision of humans convinces us we need to be wary of relying on the "goodness" of others, we have all sorts of implications about the sort of safeguards needed. Done properly, collaborative conversations can be an important safeguard that inhibits one racial group from exploiting or even oppressing others.

Both colorblindness and antiracism are secular ideologies in that they are based on the notion that we can rely on human rationality to solve racial problems. Those who promote colorblindness believe we will end racial alienation once we learn to ignore racial identity. Colorblindness is seen as the endpoint in our evolution of dealing with racism in the United States. As we become more rational, we become more convinced that race is unimportant and we learn to dismiss its importance. Political pressure can be brought to bear on holdouts who insist on making race important. Those who bring up racial issues are the problem. We must socialize them to not bring up racial conflict so we can forget about race. Once we have convinced everyone, or nearly everyone, to move beyond race, we will be able to enjoy some form of a racial utopia. The acceptance of this colorblindness will help us eventually overcome our preoccupation with race.

This is similar to the logic found among those who promote antiracism. For them the key is to teach the principles of antiracism. If we can get more people to adopt the ideals of antiracism, we will be able to move toward racial justice. Diversity training and political activism are seen as important tools for moving us toward this racial solution. Teaching whites how to support people of color is critical for ending problems connected to whiteness. While erasing the concept of race is the endpoint of evolution for those promoting color-blindness, achieving racial justice is the endpoint for those who support antiracism. They believe we can achieve a racial utopia, albeit one that looks quite different from that envisioned by those who argue for colorblindness.

While their prescriptions for solving racial problems in our society differ, both colorblindness and antiracism promote the notion that we can, in our own human ability, overcome problems such as racial alienation. Both believe that some of us can figure out the best path to racial harmony for the rest of us. Both assume that if others accept their particular ideals, society will improve. This places a high value on rationality and human ability to figure out the best path forward. Once we have figured out that path, we are obligated to socialize others to follow it. It does not matter if this socialization is not based on the ideals of moral suasion. If we have the right path, we must do all we can to make sure others go down that path—even if that means we have to rely on cultural, legal, or political power to move people down that path.

But what if we are not able to make such determinations? What if we are not able to figure out the best path forward? What if we are influenced by our own self-interest as we think through solutions for our society? What if there are forces at work that powerfully incline us to support the solutions that best serve us and the people we like? At this point we begin to understand how the biblical concept of human depravity plays an important role in helping us deal with racial alienation. Human depravity is the notion that we are not perfectible. A central message of Christianity is that we all have fallen short of perfectibility. We can, and should, strive to be better, but we must recognize we will never get there. We need Christ because of our inability to overcome our innate depravity.

This is arguably the most critical philosophical difference between Christianity and humanist approaches to reality and morality. Christians believe that humans are fallen and, depending on what a particular Christian tradition emphasizes, Christ is needed in some way to help us find our full humanity. Humanist thought is focused on obtaining full humanity through the use of human abilities rather than looking to the supernatural.

It is hard to overstate just how important this difference is when it comes to separating Christianity from secular ideologies. If we believe that human effort and ability are key to solving problems, we have a great deal of confidence in humans' ability to use rationality to solve those problems. Yes, we may acknowledge that humans do not always respond in rational ways, but that can be aided by engaging in study and thought. Once we have found the right solutions, education can be used to promote the ideals that will make our society better.

If we do not have such confidence in human ability, then we will be humbler about our ability to develop moral and ethical systems that serve all of us. If we believe we are compromised by something like human depravity, we may be especially worried about attempts to promote solutions as the "ultimate answer." We will worry that we tend to promote answers that serve us and our friends at the expense of others in our society. If human depravity is real, then having mechanisms that allow us to compensate for our depravity is critical.

SCRIPTURAL SUPPORT FOR HUMAN DEPRAVITY

I am not a professional theologian. But I can read the Bible. And it is hard to get away from the reality that our Christian faith is rooted in the notion of human depravity. How different Christian traditions define what that means varies, but there is a sense among Christians that we know we are not all we need to be. Human depravity is a concept that undergirds Christendom.

There are abundant scriptural references that point out our depravity. Romans 3:23 reminds us that all of us have sinned and fallen short of God's glory. Depravity is universal. None but Jesus has escaped it. Jeremiah 17:9 points to how sick our heart is. There is no sugarcoating the depth of depravity that lies within all of us. As a sociologist, I would argue that only powerful social norms keep our worst impulses in check. Ecclesiastes 9:3 discusses the evil and madness we live with until the day we die. Finally, 1 John 1:8-10 reminds us that our claims to goodness are lies and shows that we do not understand how depraved we have become. These and other verses highlight the pervasiveness and depth of our fallen nature. No wonder we struggle with reconciliation after centuries of racial abuse. The truth is that because of human depravity, seeking out the good of others is not in our general makeup.

Whereas the ideals of secular ideology assume that humans are basically good, the principles of human depravity teach that sin permeates the core of our lives. It is not that we cannot do anything good. Human depravity is not utter depravity; we are not as wicked as we possibly could be. But ultimately we have a desire to take care of ourselves, even at the expense of others. We will find ways to justify such actions to alleviate any potential guilt. We see this in our tendency toward confirmation bias (Nickerson, 1998), whereby we emphasize positive evidence for our beliefs even as we diminish negative evidence. Likewise, we have a bias toward facts and evidence that support our self-serving ideas and dismiss facts and evidence challenging those ideas. Left unchecked by society, personal conviction, or self-introspection, human depravity leads us toward ideas and actions that serve ourselves even if they are unfair to others.

Social movements are created by humans and subject to the same weaknesses of the humans who created them. Human depravity makes its way into social movements in the same way it enters our hearts. Social movements draw in those with similar perspectives and interests. We should expect solutions rising out of those social movements to reflect the desire of humans to latch onto ideas serving their own needs, regardless of whether they serve the needs of others. Social movements that endorse concepts such as colorblindness and antiracism simply will not succeed in eradicating the problem of racial alienation. Human depravity will prevent them from creating solutions that serve everybody; rather, the focus will be on the social interests of the particular individuals in those movements.

USING OUR UNDERSTANDING OF HUMAN DEPRAVITY TO COMBAT RACIAL ALIENATION

There may be an infinite number of differences in the ways human perfectibility and human depravity manifest themselves in our thinking. But for our concerns I will look at how a Christian response to racism can best be shaped by an understanding of human depravity. It is natural to think that unity will come about only when others do what we ask them to do. There is a confidence in those who promote their own ideals that if only everyone else would accept their perceptions, we would see an end to racial alienation. When I listen to the proponents of either perspective, I generally hear little consideration of the possibility that their approach is good for some but neglectful of the needs of others. This lack of humility does not fit with a belief in human depravity.

If we are fallen creatures, we should question our ability to devise solutions that benefit the general society. Yes, we are quite able to promote solutions that meet our needs. But our human depravity means we will not fashion solutions that address the needs of those who are not friends or allies. We will convince ourselves that our solutions are best for everyone. In essence, we will decide for those with whom we disagree about the best solutions and tell ourselves it is for their own good. This is what human depravity does. It persuades us that acting in our own best interest really is best for everyone. If we have the power to enforce our solutions on others, we feel good about using our power, because it is for their own good.

Colorblindness and antiracism are human systems in which we rely on our own intelligence and abilities to find direction. Once we have found that direction, we feel the need to compel others to follow us. Tim Keller does not use the terms *colorblindness* and *antiracism*, but he accurately describes the inadequacy of each to be the nuanced, complete solution we need given the complexity of how human depravity impacts us:

> The danger is that Christians who rightly reject the first (conservative) view as sub-biblical will merely pick up the second (progressive) view uncritically and use the terminology that it provides. But both are secular, reductionistic and simplistic. (Keller, 2020)

The overt simplicity of these models makes it easy for us to command others to follow us. Just ignore race! Just do antiracism! These appeals sound good until we truly dive into how depravity can turn such commands into new forms of mistreatment. Let us admit that we tend to deceive ourselves into thinking that what we propose is best for everyone. We should constantly engage in introspection to deal with this possibility. But even that is not likely to be enough. If we are depraved and deeply influenced by our sinful nature, even attempts at self-introspection will not be reliable. Unless we get solid input from external sources, we are likely to continue to deceive ourselves into believing we can solve our social problems with our own rationality and intellect.

So where can we get this input? As Christians we believe God provides us answers beyond our own intelligence and wisdom. But often we misinterpret God's response to us. As a sociologist, I worry that we allow our culture to tell us that God's response is not that different from what the general subculture says. We often take our own cultural values and superimpose them onto what we think God is saying to us. We repackage the gospel to fit within our subculture. Even if we do take our instruction from God correctly, we still do not live in a theocracy. We cannot force our solution onto everyone else, even if, for the sake of argument, it is indeed the perfect solution. It is not just important *that* we find good workable solutions; it is vitally important *how* we discover and promote those solutions. Christians cannot propose new directions for society as if they were given to us from God and expect everyone else in society to obey. We must have an approach that accounts for the reality of human depravity but also works for those who do not accept our faith.

While gaining insight directly through our relationship with God is valuable, we also need to find external input from sources here on earth. Looking at input from other fallen humans is a viable way to combat human depravity in a racialized society. This is especially true if we gain input from those who belong to our outgroups. If we are all fallen creatures, then interaction with other fallen creatures gives us a chance to see the excesses of our approach. That interaction can help us see where we may have, even if unintentionally, embraced perspectives that do not take into consideration the interest of others. To combat the forces of human depravity we must look with some degree of humility at the perspectives of others. We must talk and listen to them as we attempt to fashion solutions. This is the rationale for utilizing a collaborative communications approach to dealing with racial alienation in our society.

Because of human depravity, it is a mistake for us to focus so much on the goals we want to achieve that we neglect the process by which we obtain those goals. When we focus on ultimate goals, we don't realize that human depravity may be poisoning the way we envision those results. A process of collaborative communication results not only in superior solutions but also in solutions for which all interested groups have provided input. They are solutions that allow us to bring people together rather than set up a new round of recrimination and dehumanization of the opposition. If human depravity is real, dehumanization is what we should expect since we will be motivated to blame others for not accepting our approach rather than looking within to see how our approach may not benefit them. Collaborative conversation is about building community where all have input in the direction we take and where the needs of everyone are taken into account.

One of the implications of looking toward human depravity rather than human perfectibility is the role of forgiveness. Research has linked religious values and forgiveness (Fox & Thomas, 2008), and when we consider the importance of human depravity within Christianity, it is not hard to see why. If we recognize that we are fallen and come up short, then we know we need forgiveness. We do not forgive others as often as we should, but we are still reminded that forgiveness is a value we must incorporate into our lives. If done properly, forgiveness can enhance our ability to have conversations with others since it allows us to come back into conversation with those who have offended us. Knowing that forgiveness is a possibility also allows us to take chances in having meaningful conversations.

But forgiveness does not come naturally in an atmosphere where we expect perfectibility. If perfection is possible, then we have to ask the question: Why have we not reached it? The answer will vary. Marxists may argue that it is due to our capitalist system, feminists may claim it is due to sexism, and other forms of humanism offer their answers. But if human flourishing depends on ridding ourselves of barriers to perfectibility, then we can justify shaming violators of the right norms since such shaming acts as an incentive to others and moves us closer to perfectibility. In this framework it is not bad to make an example of violators of acceptable norms. If ostracizing these violators motivates others to avoid similar violations, then the pain felt by the violator is for the greater good of society. In a secular humanist framework, forgiveness can get in the way of developing the society we want.

To have the sort of dialogue we need to have about racial alienation, there will be some painful conversations. It is inevitable that some individuals will step over the line, and sometimes they will do so with malice. But we will have to find a way forward when those conversations take a turn for the worse. Cheap forgiveness is of little value. Forgiveness requires true contrition. As Christians we should be eager to accept earnestly sought forgiveness and forego holding previous sins against others. We know about our own failings and understand that we need forgiveness as well. We move forward in our racial dialogue only if people do not feel they must always walk on eggshells. Knowing that we can be forgiven if we make a mistake helps us take the risks we need to be honest. As forgiveness more naturally arises from a Christian framework than a humanist one, this ideal is another important Christian distinction that supports the use of collaborative conversations in dealing with racial alienation.

SEEKING THE GOOD OF OTHERS

While human depravity is a good way to understand why a mutual accountability approach works, we should also take into consideration another critical Christian principle: the notion that we should seek the good of others before seeking good for ourselves. We are commanded to consider the needs of others as much as, or even more than, our own needs (Philippians 2:3). It is a difficult rule to follow considering our natural inclination to seek our own interests first. I know I often fail to act according to this perspective. But it is a perspective in keeping with principles rooted in mutual accountability. As we approach conversations with others, we must ask questions about how we can aid them as well as help ourselves. Christian leadership is supposed to be servant leadership. Collaborative conversations provide us with another way in which we can serve others as we learn how to work with them to find solutions that aid them.

We can see the principle of service to others in the midst of collaborative communication in the early church. As a

multiethnic community the early church had different factions with different needs. In Acts 6:1-7 two of the factions
come into conflict, with the Grecian Jews complaining to the
Hebraic Jews about widows being overlooked. But the Hebraic
Jews were concerned about preaching of the Word. After the
groups engaged in dialogue with each other, a solution came
about that addressed the needs of both groups. Seven men
were chosen to take care of the widows, allowing the others
to tend to preaching the Word. The needs of both groups
were met as a result of collaborative communication.

To be very clear, the Bible is not merely talking about
serving people we like. We are to serve the "Samaritans" in
our lives. This is reinforced in Luke 6:32-36, which makes it
clear that we get no credit for doing good for those we love.
It is how we treat those who we see as enemies that shows our
Christian faith. How merciful we are to our enemies is more
important than how good we are to our friends. Our role
model for mercy is Jesus, who gave his life for those who hated
him. We will fall short of reaching the goal of being Christlike
in this manner, but that is our target. I know I fall short more
often than I like to admit. It is much easier to support those
who like me than those who have contempt for me. I consistently struggle and hope to improve my success rate with
more work and introspection. But striving to be counter-
cultural means going against our nature, and this is not easy.

Our human depravity motivates us to find fault with those
we do not like and to see good in those we do like. This selective way of evaluating others can feed feeling good about
our subculture's values and principles. Our nature is to seek

to punish those we hate and excuse those we like. We have a black-and-white mentality when our enemies make mistakes while seeking nuance to explain the shortcomings of our allies. We must fight against this normal human response. We must learn how to give grace to those who mistreat or misunderstand us. We must try to see issues from their perspective as well as our own. We should care about the good of those who are not like us. The Bible talks about justice. The Bible talks about equality. But the Bible also talks about mercy. Working for justice or equality must not come at the expense of the concerns of those who are not like us.

Collaborative conversations are about looking toward the needs of others and, at times, putting them before our own needs. Those conversations require us to listen and learn about the real needs of people with whom we are in disagreement and seek out solutions that meet those needs. We engage in these conversations because we want solutions acceptable to a wide number of individuals. There are practical reasons we desire such solutions, as solutions supported by many different groups will be sustainable in ways that escape imposed solutions. But there is also a spiritual reason; we are commanded to consider the needs of others at least as important as our own needs. Selfless attitudes go against our natural inclinations. Yes, there are non-Christians who put many of us Christians to shame with their willingness to give to others. But that does not diminish one iota the relevance of "dying to self" to our Christian faith. The presence of those non-Christians should simply inspire us to work harder at fulfilling the value of caring for others who are not like us.

CONCLUSION

While the Bible does not directly command us to engage in collaborative conversations or fashion a mutual accountability model, such conversations are a natural outcome of thinking deeply about our fallen nature. If we believe that humans are not perfectible but we can improve our society by recognizing our sin nature and listening to others, then we are in line with a biblical approach to intergroup conflict. However, if we consider humans perfectible and "know" how to achieve perfection, then it makes sense to concentrate on convincing everyone to accept our stated goals so we achieve that perfection. Of course, when our vision for racial harmony conflicts with the vision of others, we have continued racial strife.

I am not saying that accepting my vision of society will solve all racial problems. But let me work with you and you work with me so we can find the best solution together. I implore you to seek win-win solutions with those with whom you disagree. The difference between a Christian-based approach and a humanist-based approach is that a Christian-based approach does not force others to capitulate. A Christian-based approach desires to move individuals into healthy conversation with those with different perspectives. That difference is key to whether we will continue to have racial unrest in our society.

My faith informs me that Christians must deal with more than issues of evangelism and individual morals, as important as those issues are for us. Justice, as defined as people receiving what they deserve,[2] is also very important. But figuring out how to achieve that justice in a fair manner is difficult. I believe God knew we would face this difficulty due to our human nature. The Bible warns us about the depravity within humans, which makes it hard for us to find fair outcomes in the ways we deliver justice. That depravity incentivizes whites to ignore racial problems and people of color to make the problems bigger than they may be.

My attempt to develop a mutual accountability approach is based on my understanding of human depravity. There may be a better way to deal with depravity. I am not going to pretend I have found the ultimate solution to everything. If I believe in universal depravity, then I must believe it is in myself and my own failings can be found in my attempts at solutions. But the mutual accountability approach does take seriously the reality of human depravity. As Christians we are responsible for looking for solutions that consider humanity's sinful condition. Christians who advocate perspectives that downplay the depravity of the people they support fail to be convincing from a Christian perspective. Their attitudes cannot be differentiated from the attitudes we would expect from those who do not accept our theological perspectives.

I argue that a mutual accountability approach is uniquely Christian in origin. It is something we as Christians can offer the rest of society. In a post-Christian world (Yancey & Williamson, 2014), individuals no longer accept Christian ideals based on Christians' cultural power—and that is good. We want people to come to Christ freely rather than out of compulsion. We need to offer them something they cannot easily find outside of our ideals. Given the role human depravity plays in explaining human nature and the value of mutual accountability, this is something we can bring forward. But to make good on our offer, we need to do a better job of promoting collaborative conversations in our churches and parachurch organizations.

DOING MUTUAL
ACCOUNTABILITY
IN OUR LIVES

WHEN I THINK ABOUT LIVING a collaborative-conversations lifestyle, I think of people like Frank Byers, who graciously allowed me to interview him. Byers, who is black, grew up in a white faith-based community. He was a minister on a church staff when one of his co-ministers shared with him in a meeting that he and the church leadership had mutually discussed that he would have been a better fit for the church's growth as the worship pastor if he were white. Once those words were spoken, they could not be taken back. Two years later the leadership of the church felt he was no longer a match for what they needed and asked him to resign. His choice was not to resign, so if they wanted him out, they would have to fire him. The church leaders did so, following up their termination by sending a churchwide email that portrayed Byers as an angry black man. He was understandably upset at this chain of events.

Byers had been taught that two wrongs do not make a right, and he did not want to live in bitterness. His desire to be part of a change drove him to make a new effort at communication. Through therapists he learned about cycles we experience personally and cycles that take place in our larger society. One such cycle is police brutality followed by protests and then violence. Once violence occurs, the white community, which has the greatest power to effect change, withdraws until there is another incident. Byers soon concluded that this cycle was less about police brutality and more a reflection of the racial tension embedded in our culture. Only through heathy interracial conversations could we expose and deal with this tension.

As a principal worship leader at his current church, he started a dialogue with the music minister about intentionally scheduling worship teams that displayed racial diversity. The conversation went well. Then the Ahmaud Arbery killing occurred. He felt that the timing of this event could help him create more conversations in the church. He saw an opportunity to articulate what people of color wanted and to do it in a way that did not look like revenge, which he saw happening in secular conversations. As he was moving toward that effort, the George Floyd killing happened. Byers wondered why people were shocked since it was common for black men to be killed by police. It reinforced to him the need to promote healthy conversations.

Byers wants communities of color to see that they are not alone but also that how we handle conversation is important when dealing with whites. His strategy is to facilitate conversation, not debate. He emphasizes listening to understand. Thus when he hears whites say they do not like the phrase

Black lives matter he knows he must listen to see why they feel that way. He has problems with black organizations that try to be a voice for African Americans but also seem to tell whites to shut up. He contends that we need a dialogue, not a monologue. Whites should be able to ask questions about what it is like to be a person of color in America and not merely be told to accept everything that is said. It is not our job to bring conviction, but some organizations try to use guilt to produce conviction. A heart change will come about only with one's own decision to change. In conversation we can see our propensity to perpetuate unhealthy cycles in society and within ourselves.

Over the years listening to whites has helped Byers move away from thinking of all white people as racists. It has also helped him communicate with them. He notes that the word *racist* triggers whites similarly to how the N-word triggers blacks. While it does not have the same history, the word *racist* often causes whites to shut down. Byers realizes that while sometimes whites act in racist ways, this does not necessarily mean they are racist. Sometimes they just need to learn. As an example, he refers to the way some whites use the term *boy* when describing him. There is a racist history surrounding the word *boy* for black men, but most whites are not aware of this. Many who learn of this history change their practice.

Byers also shared with me unique insights about how politics interferes with racial dialogue when race is weaponized for political gain. He gave two examples of this. First was conservative commentator Candace Owens talking about contemporary blacks being enslaved by Democrats. Second was then–presidential candidate Joe Biden saying that if blacks did not vote for him, they were not black. This type of weaponization is bipartisan, and it interferes with real conversation. Byers's ultimate vision is to facilitate healthy dialogue that helps people understand the personal and cultural cycles in place and learn to address them. He wants to help us listen to understand and to be open and transparent, moving away from the norm of talking badly about an opponent and breaking the us-versus-them cycle. He has started a Facebook discussion group and a website (see frankbyers.com/cycle-breaking) as safe spaces for this conversation, and he is seeking to establish a nonprofit that will create tools that encourage conversation instead of debate.

Byers's experience indicates that we do not have to be trapped by experiences of racism. He turned his experience into a positive effort to make beneficial changes in society. He exhibited the ability to learn from other races and not to constrain them into boxes based on unflattering stereotypes. He has learned better communication skills from listening to whites. His efforts have led to levels of understanding that do not happen in an atmosphere of pure colorblindness or antiracism. His is a lifestyle of mutual accountability rather than a lifestyle of colorblindness or antiracism. If the efforts of men like Byers can be replicated, then we may be able to find a path out of the racial alienation that continues to bedevil us. Not all of us can be as involved as Byers, but all of us can do something. Let's keep Byers in mind as we begin to piece out what mutual accountability or collaborative conversations might look like in our own life.

A COLLABORATIVE-CONVERSATIONS LIFESTYLE

One of the obvious implications of a collaborative conversation approach is to be slow to speak and quick to listen. Note the emphasis Byers places on listening to whites and how listening helped him move away from his stereotypes. For example, he makes it a point to learn why whites feel the way they do about BLM. The value he places on listening is seen in his efforts to start a Facebook group as a safe place for conversations. Byers's life illustrates that listening is learning.

Let me say that this is more of a "do as I say" than a "do as I do" point. I often speak too quickly about issues before taking the time to listen to the perspectives of others. I do not hold myself up as the prime example of caring about the views of others. But I am trying, and I am a work in progress. I hope to continue to work at being open to listening. What would it mean if all of us worked at such an approach, as inadequate as our efforts often are? Our society would become committed to using deliberate discourse in response to racialized events. We would not just react to the first interpretation of a racial event that supported our own presuppositions, but we would attempt to understand the point of view of others as we accumulated information about the incident. It would mean that when others conducted themselves in ways of which we disapproved, we would not rush to stigmatize them with accusations of racism or of whining about race, but rather we would consider whether they had a reasonable point. We would practice generosity of spirit even as we knew we would never reach perfection.

A great example of this approach can be seen in a TED Talk by Theo E. J. Wilson (2017) titled "A Black Man Goes Undercover in the Alt-Right." In the TED Talk Wilson describes creating a social media identity as a person who supports the alt-right. As a black man he wanted to see what they were reading. Naturally a good chunk of it turned him off. Some of it was foolish. But he also found times when, surprisingly, he agreed with them. As he stated in his talk:

> I'm going to tell you what else led to the momentum of the alt-right—the left-wing's wholesale demonization of everything white and male. One thing kept screaming at me through the subtext of those arguments, and that was, why should I be hated for who I cannot help but be? Now, as a black man in America, that resonated with me. I've spent so much time defending myself against attempts to demonize me and make me apologize for who I am, trying to portray me as something that I'm not, some kind of thug or gangster or menace to society. Unexpected compassion—wow. Never in a billion years did I think that I could have some kind of compassion for people who hated my guts.

Clearly Wilson has not become an alt-right supporter. Sometimes we get the idea that understanding how others arrive at their conclusions means we agree with them. All it means is we understand their perspective and are in a better position to have a valuable conversation with them if we so desire.

Social media has become a barrier to productive conversation. Often it is used for creating interpersonal drama rather than conversations that seek resolution. If we are going to use social media to foster productive conversations, we need to be very careful how we go about it. In fact, generally I would advise not using social media for conducting collaborative conservations. However, if done carefully, we can use Facebook, Twitter, and so on to listen to the perspective of others. While this is not directly linked to racial issues, I used my Facebook page in 2016 to learn why so many of my conservative Christian friends voted for Donald Trump despite his obvious moral shortcomings and what I perceived as his incompetence. I made it clear that I wanted to hear their comments and I would only ask clarifying questions. I was not going to argue with them or tell them they made a mistake. Although it had long been clear to my Facebook friends that I was not a Trump supporter, I wanted to know why others did not see what I saw.

I found it to be a useful exercise. Like Wilson, I came to understand the rationale of those who supported Trump, even though it did not persuade me to support him. As an African American concerned about the potentially toxic effects of having Trump as president, this exercise forced me to consider why people voted for him in a way that did not just feed my own ego. Doing this helped me to see through the eyes of others and to humanize them.

Through that experiment I realized there were multiple reasons people supported Trump. Some simply preferred the policies of the Republican party. Others were concerned about the hostility they perceived in Hillary Clinton toward Christians and conservatives. Still others believed Clinton's past actions were more corrupt and immoral than anything Trump had done. Those reasons were heartfelt. They changed my approach toward Trump's supporters in coming years because it humanized them to me, even though I remained a critic of the president. This is a pattern I would like to see more of in my life—one where I attempt to understand the perspectives of those with whom I disagree on racial or even political issues rather than relying on gross stereotypes that make me feel better. Doing so would be a major way to live out mutual accountability in my interpersonal relations.

A lifestyle of mutual accountability does not mean we no longer take strong stands on issues. Of course we have passion for certain issues and want to advocate for them. But when we advocate for them, it is a mistake not to recognize the humanity of those who disagree with us. We need to recognize that we may be wrong. For this reason, as we develop our perspectives on racial issues, we should go out of our way to listen to the perspectives of others. We need to consider how we can answer others' objections and consider if there are win-win solutions. Sometimes those solutions do not exist. But I suspect they are out there more often than we realize because normally we do not look for them. We should seek such solutions out as we encounter those of different races and contrasting perspectives on racial issues.

A CONTINUING COMMITMENT

One of the reasons why some diversity efforts fail is that they are shortsighted. To change the way individuals think about racial issues, we need an ongoing commitment to employ our tools in ways that move us away from racial alienation. If the tool is mutual accountability, this means we must intentionally seek out interactions with those in other racial groups. We must be willing to engage in productive conversation with those we disagree with. We should be careful to have some degree of humility about what we do know and what we do not know and be willing to give up that which is not vital to us if it meets the vital needs of others. Let's look at these mutual accountability commitments one at a time.

We need to be committed to seeking out interracial relationships. Emerson (2010) talks about what he calls the "sixth American." What he means by this is that we tend to divide Americans into five racial groups—whites, blacks, Hispanics, Asians, and Native Americans. But he argues that there is a sixth group. This group lives a multiracial lifestyle with racially diverse friendship networks, diverse employment settings, and integrated educational institutions. Their relationship patterns do not fit within a monoracial framework but rather tend to span a variety of races. In his work on multiracial churches, Emerson argues that it is these sixth Americans who will be attracted to these churches and ensure that they thrive.

To make a commitment to mutual accountability is to become a sixth American. Such racial diversity will come naturally to some of us. As a college professor I tend to live in racially diverse college towns. Byers, a black man working in a predominantly white church, had a natural pathway toward a racially diverse lifestyle.[1] But it may not always be easy to find others of different races for relationships. We may have to go out of our way to engage in these interactions. Perhaps we attend a different church, go to different cultural events, attend public events in different communities, or use our social media to locate others with similar interests but who are of a different race. This is where commitment is important. If you only have a few token friends from different races, it is much harder to develop opportunities to engage in collaborative communication with those in other racial groups. They will remain strangers to you and your ability to understand contrasting perspectives will be curtailed.

We need to be committed to seeking out productive conversations on racial issues. Developing interracial social relationships is only part of what is necessary to develop a mutual accountability lifestyle. The truth is, it is easy to avoid racial conversations with our friends of different races or political perspectives. Our social media makes it simple for us to weed out those with dissenting opinions. When a racial incident occurs, we can run into our ideological silos and reinforce our presuppositions about what we already think is right or wrong. If we expose our racial beliefs only when we are safe in those silos, it becomes easy to fall back on gross stereotypes about our outgroups. Notice how Byers continued to seek out opportunities to talk to whites about racial issues. He did not just have white friends; he sought opportunities to teach and learn from them. To live a mutual accountability lifestyle is to be willing to have uncomfortable discussions with those of different races and outlooks.

Sometimes we think others may not understand us so we do not take the risk of talking with them. In college my best friend was white. We probably talked about every subject under the sun—except for racial issues. I did not think he would get where I was coming from on racial issues, so I did not share my thoughts with him. It was not that I did not have racial concerns. I had another friend who was not quite as close as my best friend, but he was Hispanic. I do remember discussing racial concerns with him. I was willing to develop friendships with whites but not willing to expose my racialized thoughts to them. I was being unfair to my white friend by assuming he would not be sympathetic to my racial concerns. Maybe he would not have completely understood what it was like to be a black man, but at the very least my discussion with him would have helped him know me better and could have strengthened our friendship. I did not give him the chance. So even though I may have been a "sixth American" in my social relationships, I was not living a mutual accountability lifestyle because I was unwilling to discuss racial issues with whites.

Of course, there are times when it is appropriate for us not to open our racialized selves to others. Some people may indicate they are not really interested in us or what we have to say; they are seeking only to score political or debate points on us. They are more interested in having the argument and winning the argument. There are those who seek only to convert us to their cause. They have made it clear that compromise in any form is not on the table. There are those who simply do not want to hear opinions that differ from their own. They may be uncomfortable speaking about racialized topics and a conversation will not go anywhere. Opening up to individuals such as these can not only be a waste of time but exhaust us emotionally. While people of any race can run into such barriers, they are particularly hard on people of color who have been shut out of racial conversations for so long. I am not saying that every non-black friend I have needs to hear about my racial trials. But if we have enough friends of different races and distinct perspectives on racial issues, we should inevitably have friends with whom we can have productive conversations. We must not shy away from those opportunities. We should seek them out.

However, it's also true that we may not be able to open up to those who are not also committed to a mutual accountability lifestyle. I have been personally frustrated when attempting to have conversations with people who are reflexively committed to colorblindness or antiracism. Their certainty that they have found the right path often does not allow for the productive dialogue we need to reduce racial alienation. In their minds any type of compromise will make the problem worse, not better. Productive dialogue is not possible under those conditions. We need a community of individuals committed to the principles of mutual accountability in order to engage in productive conversations. By enlarging this community, we can gain influence and move our society to a saner approach to facing racial issues.

We need to commit to being careful of our own arrogance. We all have a natural tendency to defend our own beliefs and concerns. Often those beliefs are useful in terms of meeting our social and economic needs. We often think our beliefs are objective assessments of reality and do not recognize the ways they are biased to serve us. Even if they do not directly serve our racial group, they may serve our economic or political interest. Research on confirmation bias (Lerman & Acland, 2020; Nickerson, 1998) indicates that we tend to seek out information that confirms our beliefs and dismiss evidence that challenges those beliefs. It is fine for us to acknowledge that we are biased. In fact, it is healthy for us to be honest about our inability to be objective. I appreciate Byers's efforts to move away from an us-versus-them mentality, because in that dichotomy we tend to develop an arrogance whereby our group is always right and the other group is always wrong.

Once we recognize our biases, we can have a healthy degree of humility about our confidence. We can also recognize that we should learn from the perspective of others. This does not mean we throw away our previous beliefs, but we do not hold them with an unwarranted level of certainty. We look to our interactions with others as opportunities to add to our stock of knowledge. There is a balance we must strike between holding on to our own beliefs but being open to having them changed when we encounter the ideas of others. If we refuse to consider that we may have to alter our beliefs, then we are unable to have meaningful conversations with others. Our conversations become power struggles to see who can get the other person to capitulate. But obviously shifting one's ideas at the slightest criticism is not feasible either.

Our tendency to hold to our beliefs may be even stronger when it comes to our racial attitudes. Again, our attitudes can be useful to us because they help meet our social and economic needs. They can help us gain and maintain cultural and political power. Perhaps this is why we see the vicious cycle of racial incident, protest, counterprotest, and equilibrium—it just is too challenging to consider the racial perspectives of others. We would rather engage in (counter)protest than consider if our ideological opponents have a point. A mutual accountability approach lets us move beyond that cycle precisely because it allows us to learn how to work with others and not merely argue with them.

We need to be committed to compromise when necessary. In a polarized society, compromise is often seen as a dirty word. If we see ourselves as completely correct, then why give an inch? But if we consider that we may not be correct, we can be open to the possibility that our ideas will improve when we interact with others. We can have the attitude of compromise when we perceive compromise as a way to gain better ideas, ideas that incorporate the perspectives of many others, rather than the giving up of our "correct" idea. A mutual accountability lifestyle is one where we look at receiving ideas from others as a way to improve our own ideas.

Having an attitude of compromise can also enable us to truly prioritize what is important to us. I get it. We want everything. That is a natural response we tend to take into discussions. But some things we want more than others. In normal life we make these allowances all the time. For example, I would prefer that my boys eat all their vegetables and protein without complaint. I would prefer that they minimize the amount of bread and sweets they eat. But they do not want to eat their vegetables and proteins as much as they want to eat bread and sweets. No surprise, right? So my wife and I compromise by requiring them to eat a certain amount of vegetables and protein to receive a certain amount of bread and sweets. That compromise prioritizes the fact that I want them to eat their veggies and proteins more than I want to deny them too many breads and sweets. While as a parent I can try to force them to eat the former and withhold the latter, I have learned that you must pick your battles when raising kids. Other parents may pick other battles and have different priorities about what their kids eat. That is okay. But understanding what is important for us and what our priorities are helps us know which battles to fight and how to fight them.

We also must pick our battles when dealing with racial relationships. People will resist if we insist on having everything. It is important to know what our core needs are, needs that must be satisfied for us to move forward. What can we live with and what can we live without? If the individuals we are in dialogue with also recognize what they can live with and what they can live without, it becomes a matter of trading off the nonessentials so both groups gain their essentials. It will not always work out perfectly. Sometimes what is vital for one group is also seen as vital for the other. But often we can gain the support of our ideological opponents by sacrificing something we can live without. We should ask whether it is worth it to go to war politically to get

100 percent of what we want and have 40 percent of the population fight to sabotage our gains or to engage in collaborative conversations to get 70 to 80 percent of what we want and then get to keep it, since most of the population will support our gains.

All these elements help us develop a mutual accountability lifestyle. This is a lifestyle where we make certain that all individuals involved in our ongoing racial conversations leave those conversations feeling they have been fairly treated. Where every group with an interest in a particular racialized subject has an opportunity to provide input into the solution and feel they gained something important in the final outcome. It is unrealistic to think every single person will feel this way. Some individuals will insist that any solution where they do not get everything is unfair. As humans we have a tremendous ability to rationalize receiving more than others and justifying self-serving beliefs. But if most individuals leave our encounters feeling it was a fair process and their core concerns have been addressed, then we have the potential to find sustainable solutions. Solutions that are sustainable because people from different racial and political groups have worked together to make certain the solution is viable.

As we discuss racial issues in our society, it is important to consider if we are doing so with a mutual accountability approach or a winner-take-all approach. Both the colorblindness and antiracism lifestyles are winner-take-all approaches. Those who do not surrender to the demands of either sets of advocates will not be invited to a conversation but rather will be denounced for their noncompliance. A mutual accountability lifestyle invites conversations that provide understanding of the perspectives of others and solutions that meet the needs of multiple groups, not just our own. As we interact with each other, we eventually learn to trust that the other person, while concerned about the issues at stake, is not looking to take advantage of our goodwill. Whether it is in face-to-face discussions or through social media, individuals committed to a mutual accountability lifestyle look to build bridges of communication and relationship. This way we can come to conclusions about specific racial issues in ways that eliminate barriers to understanding rather than reify our differences.

OVERCOMING OUR FEARS

Fear can keep us from a collaborative communication lifestyle—a cycle of fear that continues to poison us. Whites fear being labeled racist, which can derail careers and ruin relationships. Therefore many whites either become aggressively defensive or extremely compliant when faced with the possibility of being labeled a racist. Neither defensiveness nor compliance is useful in a collaborative conversation. People of color fear being dismissed or even ridiculed if they bring up their racial concerns. There is rejection and stigma attached to the notion of an "angry" person of color. This can lead them to either be aggressive in asserting their demands or simply refuse to speak up. Neither response is useful in the development of productive communication.

This cycle of fear inhibits our recovery from racial abuse. Whites' fear leads them to ignore racial issues. Their efforts to dismiss those issues feed into the fears of people of color that their concerns about racism will not be taken seriously. Thus people of color increase their support for leaders who foolishly play the race card, whereby members of a racial minority use racism accusations to gain leverage in a situation but who take seriously concerns about racial justice. Playing the race card and similar acts only increase the fears of whites because they become concerned they will be labeled as racist no matter what they do. As whites' fears intensify, they increase their efforts to push for colorblindness, which then exacerbates the fears of people of color. And the cycle of fear continues, deepening with each revolution through the cycle, and our dysfunctional race relations just deteriorate as we talk past each other instead of to each other.

Figure 1. Cycle of dysfunctional racial relationships

To whites I must say that, yes, if you engage in racial conversations, you run the chance of being accused of being a racist. Sometimes there may be merit to the accusation. At other times someone will be playing the race card. But you must push through that fear. Defensiveness may feel like a natural and justifiable response, but be open to the possibility that you have offended others regardless of your intentions. If you take that attitude, you will learn when the accusations are real and when they are intended to manipulate. The relationships you develop with people of color will not only provide you with enlightenment, but those very people will defend you when you are unfairly accused. However, if you let your fears dominate you, then not only will you fail to learn from people of color; they also will not understand your fears of being labeled a racist. You will deprive both yourself and them of the chance to learn. Instead of your fears going away, they will only grow in the absence of honest interactions with people of color.

To people of color, I know where you are coming from. I too tire of bringing up my concerns only to have them shot down by whites who really do not care about them or me. I have learned through trial and error who I can and cannot talk to about racial issues. When I can talk to someone, I am able to learn about their perspectives and engage in real conversation. I am not looking for a one-way conversation where I simply tell them what I want. I need to know what troubles them and how we can find ways to help each other. But that can happen only when I am willing to engage with them in ways that allow them to hear me. Not in overt or passive aggression but rather in relationship and frank dialogue. Every time I have a successful conversation, I become more encouraged that we can figure our way out of this racial mess. But if I do not allow for this type of collaborative conversation, I am left with my fear that whites will not take me seriously. Some will not. But I have learned that many will, and I need to move beyond my fear so I can work with them.

We cannot let our fears inhibit us from collaborative conversations. The source of fear for whites and nonwhites is different, but the solution to dealing with those fears is the same. The key is for both whites and people of color to move beyond their fears and work with each other. We must lean in to the solution of collaborative conversation. The "other" side will always seem strange and scary if they are unknown to us. Ironically, the way to make sure our fears do not interfere with a collaborative communications lifestyle is to engage in collaborative communications.

FEARS IN OUR BROKEN RELATIONSHIPS

Let me tell you a story. There were a man and woman who were married in a land where divorce was illegal. They were married for fifteen years. But it was a horrible marriage. The husband was very abusive to his wife. His abuse was mental, physical, and even sexual. The wife withstood this horrible situation for as long as she could. At the end of those fifteen years, she told him she had had enough. Even if she could not legally leave the marriage, she decided she would aggressively protect herself from her husband from that point on. In that moment the husband realized how awful he had been. He decided he would not be abusive anymore. He told his wife he would stop his pattern of abuse. And he did. So the couple lived happily ever after.

Wait, that is not realistic. Does anyone think a marriage that has endured fifteen years of violent abuse will become normal simply because the abuser stops? The relational and psychological damage that has occurred must be accounted for if that marriage has any chance of surviving. The most logical outcome to this story is that the wife will still protect herself from the husband and keep him at bay. She will be left with unresolved anger and bitterness at all the years she has lost in this terrible relationship.

So let us try again. There were a man and a woman who were married in a land where divorce was illegal. They were married for fifteen years. But it was a horrible marriage. The husband was very abusive to his wife. His abuse was mental, physical, and even sexual. The wife withstood this horrible situation for as long as she could. At the end of those fifteen years, she told him she had had enough. Even if she could not legally leave the marriage, she decided she would aggressively protect herself from her husband from that point on. In that moment the husband realized how awful he had been. He decided he would not be abusive anymore. He told his wife he would stop his pattern of abuse. And he did. But naturally that was not enough for the wife. Because of all the damage he had done to her, she demanded that he learn about the needs of abused women. She forbade him from replying back to her when they had arguments. She was free to hound and berate him and command him to do what she wanted for at

least the next fifteen years since she had spent fifteen tor-
turous years with him. He saw her request as fair in light of
the terrible way he had treated her, so now they could have a
happy marriage and move forward.

Wait a minute. I do not believe this one either. Do you?
Yeah, the guy is awful and does not deserve his wife. But will
taking away his sense of autonomy really make this a livable
situation? Do we really believe that those who have been victimized cannot then go on to victimize others? If that were
true, why do abused children often grow up to be abusers
themselves? Creating new rules assuming that a victimized
person cannot become a victimizer is not the way forward
either. This relationship is likely to become poisonous in different ways than before unless we take seriously the responsibilities of both parties to deal with their inner demons.

In the context of our racial history and contemporary situation, the meaning of the analogy is clear. Whites have historically abused people of color, and today there is a reckoning
about that abuse. People of color can now make demands
and be heard in ways that were not possible in the past. Yet
this new phase of equality and justice does not seem to be
healing our wounds. The example of the awful marriage indicates why this is the case. Fear is undoing efforts to save the
marriage. In the first case the husband has stopped the abuse
but the wife knows his potential to start abusing her again.
How can she be assured he will continue to treat her right?
Does he truly feel remorse for what he has done or is he
merely putting on a show to keep her placated? Is he willing
to take action to compensate for the pain she has

experienced at his hands? The husband's nonproactive reaction only slightly lessens the wife's fears. She is not currently being abused, but he gives no other indication of being a changed man who wants to make things right.

But fear is not a one-way process. The husband also has fears inhibiting the potential healing in the relationship. The actions of the wife in the second scenario feed into those fears. Will the wife use her newfound status to seek revenge instead of justice? Will he be allowed to have a say in the direction of the marriage or will he forever be punished for his past? Is he opening himself up to emotional manipulation due to his confession? These concerns do not mitigate the husband's responsibly to compensate for the damage he has done to the relationship, but they are legitimate concerns and if not addressed can result in the relationship falling apart. In both cases the cycle of fear continues to poison the married couple's relationship long after the abuse has ended.

So let us try this one last time. There were a man and woman who were married in a land where divorce was illegal. They were married for fifteen years. But it was a horrible marriage. The husband was very abusive to his wife. His abuse was mental, physical, and even sexual. The wife withstood this horrible situation for as long as she could. At the end of those fifteen years, she told him she had had enough. Even if she could not legally leave the marriage, she decided she would aggressively protect herself from her husband from that point on. In that moment, the husband realized how awful he had been.

But that was not enough. The husband and wife had built up a decade and a half of dysfunctional relationship patterns that needed to be reformed. The husband had the lion's share of the work to change his ways. Not only did he have to refuse to engage in abusive behavior, he had to learn patience and sensitivity to the needs of his wife. His years of abuse had taken away his right to engage with his wife in ways other men could with their wives. He had to go the extra mile to work toward regaining her trust. In his communication with her, he began to learn and appreciate the work he needed to do.

But the wife also had work to do. She had to deal with her anger in healthy ways so it did not fester. She learned that her desire for revenge had to be contained and that engaging her husband in healthy conversation was better for the long-term health of their relationship than manipulating his feelings of guilt. Indeed, through this careful communication, she learned when her reactions were justifiable and based on reasonable fears and when they were unfair emotional blackmail. Now, and only now, after a lot of hard work and tough communication with each other, could the couple re-build the damaged marriage. Now they were able to establish a relationship of mutual respect and love. Now it became possible for them to have a livable marriage. The route to make the marriage livable would require intentional efforts to rebuild the damaged relationship.

By using this analogy I am not saying a woman must stay in an abusive relationship. In the real world sometimes abuse is so great that the marriage is not salvageable. But divorce is not really an option for race relations. Are we going to follow

Marcus Garvey's "Back to Africa" program? Separate our country into white, black, Hispanic, Asian, and Native American areas? Since separation is not an option, we must choose the direction we will go. Do we take the first path, which represents colorblindness and focuses on ignoring racial issues? Do we take the second path, which represents antiracism and prioritizes the needs of people of color over that of whites? Or do we take the third path, which is built on the mutual accountability model and holds that communication and respect are the only ways we will overcome the fears that threaten to keep us apart?

In the book *More Than Equals* (2000), Spencer Perkins and Chris Rice discuss a potential breaking point in their ministry. White Christians had come to serve in an African American inner city area. The whites believed they were doing those blacks a service, but they took up the leadership roles themselves. Given our society's racial history and the lack of voice for African Americans, this led to conflict. The tension threatened to end the relationship in "divorce." But in communication with each other the group found compromises that allowed for a more diverse leadership team. They overcame their fears and instead of separating from each other, they built a stronger organization. Deliberate efforts at productive conversation are necessary if we are going to heal the racial damage in our society.

IN IT FOR THE LONG HAUL

Centuries of overt racial abuse followed by decades of racial mistrust will not be soon overturned. Those who expect a mutual accountability lifestyle to immediately remove the effects of our racial history are in for a rude awakening. Undoing the damage will take time and persistence. I wish I could tell you how long it will take, but no one knows. No one can say exactly when we will have "arrived" in our quest for a better racial world. There is no easy answer to questions like this. Persistence is the order of the day.

There will be failures. Some may be spectacular. Forged compromises will sometimes break down. When they do, we should expect proponents of colorblindness and antiracism to tell us they told us so. Individuals wedded to these perspectives have a strong incentive to popularize any setbacks we face in promoting mutual accountability. At times we will attempt to engage in dialogue with those who are not ready for it. There will be great frustration as some will take advantage of our goodwill and efforts to understand their perspective. We will have to keep getting off the mat and trying again. What choice do we have? Do we just give in to the demands from colorblind proponents to ignore race? Do we surrender to the antiracists and shut down the perspectives of the majority group? I wish I could tell you that following this path will never result in falling down, but to state such a claim is to set you up for even greater disappointment when failures occur.

Those who adopt a mutual accountability lifestyle must make a commitment not to give up. We must steel ourselves for the challenges that lie ahead. If collaborative conversation is the best way forward, we must persist even when it seems we are making no progress. I admit I have not always wanted to forge ahead on days when it seemed like nobody wanted to hear it. But it has been heartening to see more interest in these ideas of late. Persistence in pursuing collaborative communication can one day help us break the cycle of racial incident, protest, counterprotest, and normalcy as we head toward a world where we can work together to solve our racialized problems.

TOWARD A LARGER MOVEMENT OF MUTUAL ACCOUNTABILITY

WHEN I WROTE ABOUT MY RACIAL CONCERNS IN 2006, people asked me if there were organizations doing anything like what I was describing. Unfortunately I had to tell them no. I did not know of any organizations that utilized collaborative communication to deal with racial issues. I assumed such organizations existed, but since I had not found them, I could not recommend any.

Fortunately, that is no longer the case. The organization Game Changer (see gamechanger1.org) now fits the bill. Game Changer is based in Los Angeles. The events leading up to its formation occurred in 2014 and 2015, when a spate of unarmed black men were shot and killed by white male police officers. Sean Sheppard, the founder of Game Changer, noted the political activity related to issues of same-sex marriage. He remembers many people on Facebook turning their profile pictures into the rainbow flag. But while an overwhelming majority of his white friends and acquaintances turned their profile pictures into the rainbow flag, they said absolutely nothing about African Americans like himself being killed by the police. He found the silence was nearly as distressing as the killings themselves.

After a period of venting and praying Sheppard knew he needed to address this problem in ways other than complaining. He decided to lean in to his life experiences as an athlete and coach to bring together law enforcement, community residents, and elected officials in the same way sports bring together many different kinds of people. Sheppard created a white paper and began circulating it to individuals whose personal and professional opinions he respected. One of those people was police chief of the San Diego Police Department, with whom he had a relationship based on a shared sports background. The chief read the white paper and said, "I get it. I believe this can work. Let's do it."

On December 12, 2016, the first Game Changer event took place at the KPBS television station on the San Diego State University campus, three hours before the start of the SDSU men's basketball game. Since then Sheppard has conducted training events across the country. At these trainings, participants arrive three hours before a major sports event. They complete a pre-event survey measuring their attitudes toward the police and citizens. A moderated focus group discussion takes place among members of the community, law enforcement, and other interested parties. The participants next fill out a post-event survey right after the discussion and then attend the game or entertainment event. Five weeks after the event, the participants receive another survey to fill out. All surveys are then analyzed to determine whether participants' views have shifted as a result of the training and discussion.

Game Changer is accredited by the California Commission on Peace Officer Standards and Training (POST). Participating California officers with a POST ID number receive continuing education units in community policing and interpersonal communication. There has yet to be any peer-reviewed research on the program, but the surveys have been analyzed and indicate tremendous promise. An independent analysis by the San Diego State University Institute of Public Health indicates that in 2018, 94 percent of general public participants had a more positive view of law enforcement after the event, and 85 percent of law enforcement participants had a more positive view of the general public. Whites generally had more favorable views of law enforcement in both pre- and post-event surveys than people of color, but the difference narrowed after the Game Changer event. In a 2020 analysis, 71 percent of general public participants had a more positive view of law enforcement, and 68 percent of law enforcement had a better understanding of community members of color. In both years general public participants reported making more balanced comments about law enforcement on social media, while law enforcement participants reported initiating more casual communication with civilians in the community.

The preliminary results of Game Changer are exciting, and it is what we would expect according to what research has indicated about a collaborative communication approach.

Until we have more evidence we cannot know the full potential of such efforts at collaborative communication, but given these preliminary results, it appears valuable for our society to develop more organizations like Game Changer. It is my hope that Game Changer will continue to enjoy success and serve as an example of a path out of racial alienation. But it also reminds us that attempts to move toward a collaborative conversation approach cannot be limited to individual efforts. It cannot even be limited to organizations such as Game Changer. We need to strengthen entire communities with these new norms and values. We must develop institutions at many levels of our society that move down this path.

Only through coordination with like-minded individuals and larger institutions can we break through the intellectual duopoly of colorblindness and antiracism. One of the reasons those ideologies persist is that they are embedded in social structures that are greater than charismatic individuals. Those structures keep the ideals alive regardless of the individuals who help promote them. In this final chapter I want to consider how we can move the ideas of mutual accountability and collaborative conversation from the drawing board to reality. To compete with the social movements supporting colorblindness and antiracism, we need a social movement promoting the ideals of mutual accountability. This means institutions must commit to employing collaborative communication techniques to address racial concerns. It also means we must create an atmosphere of social support for those seeking a new path. It is not enough to make the argument about why mutual accountability is the best way to go. We must put into place the social mechanism to make it a reality.

SEEKING SOCIAL SUPPORT

Going against the current stream of cultural thought is not easy. When everyone else holds a certain opinion, it's easy to question whether you have come to the right conclusion. I have always been one willing to think outside the box, but even I get tired of having my sanity, loyalty, and intelligence questioned. We currently live in a colorblindness/antiracism world. Those are the only two alternatives most people tend to recognize. Introducing a third option means that at least for a time many will question our adherence to a deviant choice. To this end it is valuable for us to find like-minded individuals who can provide us with social support to help us move forward in our convictions.

It is vital to build up a community of individuals willing to support each other as we promote a different path. It used to be that to find community we looked only to those living in our immediate neighborhoods and cities. Technology has removed this barrier, especially in a day of the internet. Now like-minded individuals can find each other online. We must take advantage of these new opportunities if we are going to find the social support we need. To that end, I have established a Facebook group called Collaborative Conversations and Race to help facilitate such interactions. The use of social media is important in contemporary society to foster support for a social movement that does not yet enjoy wide public awareness.

Online visibility allows supporters of collaborative conversations to have a voice and find fellow travelers of the third path. Another important strategy is for those with writing ability to develop online articles and blogs that promote the idea of collaborative conversations. Most of us do not have the opportunity to present our work to a large number of individuals. Perhaps our ideas will be read by just a few individuals. But each article or blog will boost the presence of mutual accountability among the general public. Such work will also allow for more discussion of the nuances of implementing these ideas as well as theories about the ways mutual accountability can potentially benefit our society.

While the internet is invaluable for helping to connect people, this does not mean personal contact can be ignored. Personal friendships that go beyond the screen bring about essential and fulfilling interactions. In my personal life, interaction with those in Christian communities has been invaluable for helping me develop and promote the concepts I believe in. I am grateful for the opportunity to connect with many churches that are interested in mutual accountability. There is a strong theological basis for these ideas, and many churches find that these principles help them direct their members toward solutions that fit within their belief systems. These churches can also operate as vessels that provide social support for proponents of collaborative conversations. An organization that makes a commitment to the approach outlined in this book will naturally attract more individuals who are committed to the ideals of collaborative communication. Such organizations make it easier for individuals committed to collaborative conversations to find each other and flourish together.

Of course, religious institutions should not be the only social institutions that provide a meeting place for those committed to collaborative communication. Any organization where membership is voluntary can become a place of support. There is nothing to stop supporters of mutual accountability from forming their own voluntary civic or social organizations that support these ideals even if the organization's primary focus is another cause. When I studied multiracial churches, I often found that these churches focused on some other goal rather than racial diversity, but diversity rose out of their attempts to meet that goal. For example, Catholic churches tend to focus on serving their neighborhood, and if that neighborhood is racially diverse, members of that congregation become motivated to making their church multiracial. Likewise, organizations that promote community welfare may find it useful to support mutual accountability, since this approach can aid them in serving their community.

Finally, any social movement needs a certain level of organization. It needs individuals who can keep records about activities as well as records about who may be able to support the movement. Such information can be used to make strategic decisions that move the group forward in a rational manner. Unfortunately, organization is not a strong suit of mine. While I recognize the importance of such efforts, I was not blessed with the abilities to implement organizational tactics. However, in addition to developing a Facebook page for those interested in dialogue on this subject, I have also started the Baylor Program for Collaborative Conversations and Race (see ccr.baylorisr.org). The purpose of this program is to facilitate research on the potential of collaborative conversations to lessen racial tension and also to develop a network of individuals and organizations that desire to promote collaborative conversations as a solution. I hope the Facebook page and the Baylor program are only the first of many such organizations.

DEVELOPING RESOURCES

I have observed a certain phenomenon several times. Individuals become passionate about a racial issue. They want to find solutions that reduce hate crimes or prevent police shootings or increase representation for people of color in important institutions. So they look for resources to help them achieve their goals. When they look for those resources, they face the clear reality that those resources are dedicated mostly to antiracism causes. So if those individuals want to be proactive in dealing with their particular racial cause, it is difficult for them to move in a direction other than antiracism. We must develop alternative resources so that these individuals have a choice about whether they use antiracism or utilize a mutual accountability approach that can bring together the perspectives of individuals across the racial and political terrain to find win-win solutions. Those individuals may choose to stick with antiracism, but at least they will have an opportunity to move away from it if they so choose.

Obviously financial resources are important. Finding individuals and institutions that will fund an antiracism effort is much easier than finding those who will fund efforts at collaborative communication. The mere fact that eight billion dollars a year is spent on diversity training indicates the availability of money out there for dealing with our dysfunctional race relations. But until the ideology of mutual accountability becomes better known and we have more evidence of its success, it will not be easy to find financial support for collaborative communication efforts. Developing a platform that allows more individuals to know about the value of collaborative communication will likely bring this movement to the attention of those who may be able to help it financially.

As important as money is in helping those who want to deal with racialized problems, other resources are just as essential. Whenever there is a racial incident, the media quickly rushes to find advocates of antiracism or, on more conservative outlets, colorblindness to put on the air. We need to find convincing spokespeople who can promote the ideas of mutual accountability to the general public. I am grateful for opportunities to speak to audiences on the value of collaborative communication, but I know that there must be more individuals promoting these issues in the public domain. We need to find articulate disseminators of the principles discussed in this book and ideally place some of those communicators on popular media television programs and influential podcasts.

Speaking of the media, the written word is also a venue we need to take seriously. For some, written material that is on pages instead of screens will carry more weight. Books and articles that move us away from the colorblindness-antiracism duopoly should be supported even if they do not promote all the features of collaborative conversations.[1] The more individuals can showcase the inadequacies of colorblindness and antiracism in carefully constructed arguments, the more others will be open to the alternative of mutual accountability. Not only do we need books that make the case for collaborative communication, we need written work that informs us how to make these values work in racial situations. We need written work on how to negotiate stalemates in racial discussions, how to understand the perspectives of racialized cultures, and the best practices for listening and communicating with others—all these are topics that would benefit from more analysis.[2] Of course, this is not an exhaustive list of potential topics, but it should get us started thinking about developing a critical mass of thinkers who write on collaborative conversations as a solution to racial alienation.

Beyond working toward public promotion of mutual accountability, it is also vital that we create academic resources. Academic legitimation provides important cultural support for social movements. Earlier I pointed out research indicating the inadequacy of colorblindness and antiracism approaches to either reflect racial reality or offer workable solutions. Nevertheless, some academics (Ajunwa, 2020) argue for antiracism by stating that companies have not gone far enough, but they do not supply solid evidence that antiracism programs worked in the first place. In fact, systematic assessments of antiracism indicate that it has failed.

What we do not yet have is research that directly shows the power of collaborative communication to alter racial attitudes and actions. There is good work indicating its power in dealing with interpersonal conflict but little if any evidence showing that such an approach will succeed in racialized conflict. If I believe that collaborative communication is superior to antiracism or colorblindness—and I do believe that—then I believe that well-designed research will produce findings supporting those beliefs. I want to see such work done as soon as feasible.

Such research would provide an academic basis for cultural support of a mutual accountability social movement. Think about how often individuals cite peer-reviewed research to justify their perspective on a given issue. While most articles in peer-reviewed journals and books do not gain heavy readership, they can be the basis of popular articles read more extensively and have a disproportionate impact on the opinions of others. Research indicating that collaborative communication is a viable method for dealing with racial alienation can be featured in online and print articles and force supporters of colorblindness and antiracism to defend their assertions in the academic realm. In my perfect world we would have a group of committed social scientists from several disciplines fully exploring the efficacy of a mutual accountability approach and writing in academic and popular venues.

Finally, let's not forget that time and effort are important resources. The more individuals who become convinced that collaborative conversation is a better approach than colorblindness or antiracism, the more individuals we will have posting supportive messages, talking to friends and family members about this approach, and moving their organizations toward this model. I am grateful to have worked with and be working with several churches that want to seek an approach that avoids the pitfalls of colorblindness and antiracism.[3] I am also grateful to be in contact with some members of the military who are searching for better solutions.[4] These opportunities come about only because individuals within those groups are willing and able to influence their institutions toward the potential of collaborative communication.

ROBBING PETER TO PAY PAUL

To gain resources for a collaborative communication movement, we will need to persuade some who support antiracism or colorblindness to look at mutual accountability instead. There is value in gaining resources from those who have looked at both approaches and found them wanting. I believe they are a natural audience for a movement toward mutual accountability.

To this end we can attract individuals like Jeremy Pierce.[5] Pierce grew up in a mostly white suburban town without much ethnic diversity. So it is not surprising that colorblindness made sense to him as an ideal way to look at race relations. He remembers hearing a speaker talk about how race did not matter, and that seemed right to him. However, in college he became aware of the issues racial minorities faced, especially his Asian and Asian American roommates. One particularly impactful discussion occurred while they were watching the television show *Get Smart.* This particular episode poked fun at an Asian stereotype, which his roommate found offensive. This and other events helped Pierce become aware of the ways people of color could be affected. It helped him move away from colorblindness and become more firmly committed to seeing diversity as beneficial. This belief was strengthened as Pierce observed different cultural aspects of the campus ministries he attended.

In the third year of Pierce's doctoral program, his adviser offered a class called Race and Identity. While taking the class Pierce also became engaged to a black woman. These situations prompted him to think about racial classifications more deeply. The course also exposed him to several viewpoints that further challenged his assumptions. He eventually accepted that race is real but not biological, and he wrote a paper that impressed the professor, who wanted him to follow up on it for presentation and publication.

Pierce was initially looking to pursue other directions in his academic training, but those plans fell apart when key professors left his program. Eventually he sought out the professor of his Race and Identity class and created a dissertation proposal on the topic recommended by that professor. Working on his dissertation exposed him more deeply to the ideas of critical race theory and antiracism in an academic setting. It was a diversity trainer he encountered in his doctoral research who introduced him to the term *antiracism* for the first time. At first, he saw antiracism as simply being opposed to racism. But he found that the trainer was using the term in a particular way—one with which he did not completely agree. The trainer's material was particularly worrisome because it carelessly assumed racist intent in actions and events that could have been based on other motives. Pierce became concerned with how the trainer presented ideas and found, through this individual, an entire community with the same dysfunctional point of view.

In his view, many of the problems of antiracism were due to uncharitable interpretations in which everything was done to maintain power and white privilege. Pierce also saw a problem with linking negativity to the definition of whiteness. His black wife—who, ironically, tended to be more conservative on racial issues than he—gave him a book by John McWhorter. He found himself persuaded by McWhorter's refusal to read race into everything.

Pierce never became comfortable with antiracism, although he did become convinced that certain ideas concerning systematic racism were accurate. He also became comfortable with standpoint epistemology to a certain degree.[6] But he decided to avoid using terms such as *systematic racism* given that individuals tend to link racism to personal animosity, which he does not feel. Likewise, while he finds use for terms such as *white privilege* and *intersectionality*, he believes they are too often misapplied and taken too far.

While conducting his research, one of Pierce's main concerns was the way antiracism-framed discussions prevented people from being able to talk with each other. He noted that academics often say radical things but tend to dial it back when confronted. However, social media users pick up those ideas, which reveals their toxicity. He saw antiracism proponents on Twitter and Facebook attempt to shut off dialogue and observed how that affects race-related interactions. He eventually joined a Facebook group started by someone who shares many of his concerns and found himself in the middle of debates on how to move forward in our racialized society. He encountered opponents of critical race theory (CRT) who did not see any value in it because of the toxic ways it is often expressed. But he felt that their critiques largely missed the mark even as he developed his own concerns about CRT.

Today Dr. Pierce focuses on not shutting down conversations, of which those promoting colorblindness and those promoting antiracism are both guilty. Instead, it is important to work at understanding the perspectives of other individuals. In his training as a philosopher he learned to focus on being charitable with others about their ideas—trying to see ideas, even those we disagree with, in the best possible light. Doing so is important since we all have a moral responsibility to make the world better. Everyone will be better off if we work together to overcome our racial divisions, so we should care about what others want and do our best to learn from them—and hopefully they from us.

In Pierce we see someone who wants to find a way out of this racial mess we have created. We see someone who is committed to taking deliberate steps to deal with our racialized society instead of ignoring the enduring effects of racism. But he finds for a variety of reasons that antiracism is not a viable path. How many people are there who want to do something but cannot intellectually or emotionally deal with the excesses found in the antiracism agenda? I do not have hard data on such a question, but I am willing to wager that it is not a small number. Finding them and learning how we can work together is an important task if we are going to strengthen a movement toward mutual accountability.

POLITICAL ACTIVISM?

It is possible that a mutual accountability response is not as amenable to political activism as colorblindness or antiracism. Part of the difference for those of us who support a mutual accountability model as opposed to colorblindness or antiracism is that we do not believe we have all the final answers. We believe that those answers come about only as we consult each other to figure out solutions that work for us all. The art of politics requires individuals to promote ideas that will lead to laws and policies, and political activism involves promoting ideas as final solutions. Thus it is easy to use conservative political activism to push ideas that enfranchise colorblindness into our law and policies or to use progressive political activism to push ideas that enfranchise antiracism into our law and policies. This sort of political clarity is not immediately evident within mutual accountability.

But this does not mean there is not a place for political activism in a mutual accountability model. I do not anticipate that we will take to the streets and make political demands. However, the process of constructing laws and policies helps make certain our solutions pull us together rather than rip us apart. I anticipate that much of our political participation will be to make certain all voices are heard. We will be concerned about efforts to impose solutions before all interested parties have been consulted. We will also encourage our governmental institutions and private organizations to incorporate collaborative conversation into diversity efforts. It is not that we do not care about the final decisions on how the government handles racialized concerns. I know I do. But those of us committed to finding win-win solutions know that if we try to impose our own desires without working with others, we are setting up those final solutions for continued challenge and sabotage by political opponents. So while there are elements I want to see in the solutions put forward by our government, I am willing to give up on some of those elements to get the core of what I want. Especially if making such a compromise allows me to gather support from those who do not naturally support my particular solution.

This will put us at odds with efforts to impose antiracism diversity programs on public educational institutions. The philosophy of antiracism does not lend itself to collaborative communication. Its efforts are geared toward convincing individuals of a certain ideology rather than helping them learn to communicate with others and find solutions that meet the needs of different groups. We want to promote an educational system that teaches individuals how to think critically and consider the perspectives of others. Some of the information I have presented about how to persuade others and engage in active listening should be taught to our students and featured in diversity training in the public arena. The type of diversity training we support would challenge all of us to deal with our biases and presuppositions by improving our critical thinking skills and interpersonal communication skills.

Given the concerns of mutual accountability, it just does not seem likely to me that we will find supporters of collaborative communications who are highly active in political protest. The sort of confidence that says we have the final answer is not part of what our ideology is about. But I do see us communicating with political officials and using institutional influence to help shape the process by which racialized decisions are made. I anticipate that we will use books and speeches to put our ideas about reform into the public sphere. We will work behind the scenes and use moral suasion to influence political officials. This is the sort of political activism I anticipate for those who support a mutual accountability model.

MOVING FORWARD

We have come to the end of this book. I have made my case for a different, and in my view better, way to deal with racial issues beyond colorblindness or antiracism. So I think one of three things must have happened by now. First, you may have concluded that my arguments are insufficient for changing your mind about racial issues. You may have started this book with the idea that the best way to deal with racial issues is to ignore race and treat everyone the same. My arguments about the enduring impact of racism and contemporary forms of racial discrimination have failed to move you. You will continue to advocate for a colorblind perspective as the answer to racial problems. Or you started this book sympathetic to antiracism, and you remain unconvinced that antiracism produces unbalanced solutions or that its solutions do not work. You believe that my approach is not fair or considerate of the plight of people of color. And so you will keep fighting for antiracism solutions. If either of these is the case, then all I can say is God bless and I wish you well. Obviously we are limited in how we can work together to deal with racial issues in our society.

Second, you may have come to this book feeling dissatisfied with one of those two perspectives or somewhat knowledgeable about collaborative communication. You like some of what you have read but still have concerns about certain assertions or the implications of my claims. You may not be comfortable with either colorblindness or antiracism, but you may not yet be comfortable with a mutual accountability approach either. That is fair. Our racialized society offers complex dilemmas not easily resolved. I hope my presentation of this alternative at least provides enough information for you to consider other paths toward reducing racial alienation in our society. If you have concerns about a mutual accountability approach, I hope you continue to explore them. In time I hope you will see the value of collaborative conversations in dealing with racial conflict and find a place within a social movement promoting this solution.

Finally, there are those of you who have come to the book already considering an alternative to either colorblindness or antiracism or know this is the best approach for you. If that is you, I welcome you to this journey. It is one I have taken up for myself and I know it is a long-term commitment. I have no illusion that we will overcome the well-established dominance of colorblindness and antiracism within our society in the near future. But if mutual accountability is a superior path, then it is worth the time and effort we will put into promoting it for the larger society. I want to encourage those who have become convinced of the worth of collaborative conversation in dealing with racial issues. Consider my advice on living a mutual accountability lifestyle and consider supporting organizations such as Game Changer and the Baylor Program for Collaborative Conversations and Race. We need to work ourselves to become better listeners and communicators, to develop organizations that promote collaborative conversations, and to influence current social institutions so they are more open to using such types of communication.

My desire is that this last group will grow. I hope we will not be starry-eyed and think making changes will be easy or happen all at once. But persistence is a valuable commodity in such struggles. As we build networks and locate resources for promoting a mutual accountability approach, we will also build a community of individuals committed to those changes. Indeed, the relationships we form in those communities can be examples for others about how we learn to communicate with each other to solve problems. I hope you seek ways to join that community and work with us. I believe we can make a difference. If I did not have that belief, I would not have put the time into this project. Working together, we can help our society become one where we listen to each other and our communication leads us to the win-win solutions that truly fulfill the promise of our multiracial society.

As you consider my challenges, I want you to think about these words from Martin Luther King Jr. (1962):

People fail to get along because they fear each other; they fear each other because they don't know each other; they don't know each other because they have not communicated with each other.

Folks, we know what works in our personal lives. We know that when we have interpersonal conflict, we cannot ignore it or just shut the other person up. Those paths lead merely to fearing one another. We must find ways to communicate with those with whom we are in conflict to find solutions and move forward. Why would we think our solutions to racial strife would be any different? Do you want to keep working with movements that ignore our racial problems or shut down healthy conversations, or do you want to be part of the movement that is about communication? If you want to be part of the solution, then join that last group and let's take this journey together.

ACKNOWLEDGMENTS

IN SOME WAYS THIS BOOK has been thirty years in the making. I know that once I start thanking people for the way they impacted me, I will leave some of them out. But one has to try anyway. I am so grateful for my ongoing friendship with Michael Emerson. God brought him into my life at just the right time to help me learn deeply about race relations in ways that would otherwise have escaped me. In those early years there were others who helped give me insight. My relationships with those such as Mark DeYmaz, Keith Atkinson, Alvin Bibbs, Chris Rice, and the late Spencer Perkins, as well as the writings of the likes of David Anderson, Brenda Salter McNeil, Curtiss DeYoung, and Alvin Sanders, helped me formulate my ideas. **Of course, do not blame them for any mistakes you detect in my thinking.**

I have far too many modern influences to mention. But I am thankful for the opportunity to go to graduate school and develop my sociological imagination. I am blessed that God gave me a mind that does not allow itself to be trapped by conventional ideas. One's ideas are not right merely because they are different from other ideas. But being willing to challenge what is perceived as common wisdom often brings insights that are easily missed.

I can honestly say that this book would not have been possible without the encouragement given to me by my dear wife, Drommie. She saw the need for this book at a time like this. Her support provided me the motivation and willingness to put these ideas out there. Anyone who benefits from this work owes her a debt of gratitude, as do I. Finally, my greatest motivation, besides striving to be obedient to my Lord, are my three boys—George Leonard, James Mitchell, and Charles Lyndon. I write to create a better world for them and to show them that what we do can, and must, make a difference.

NOTES

1. WE NEED A NEW PATH

[1]The declining support of whites for beliefs in innate racial superiority has been documented as far back as twenty-five years ago (Schuman, Steeh, Bobo, & Krysan, 1997). Indeed, most researchers have stopped including questions connected to supremacist beliefs because so few individuals will overtly support such statements. Thus race scholars have theorized about modern forms of racism that are not reliant on white supremacy beliefs (Bonilla-Silva, 2006; Perry, 2007).

[2]Indeed, right before I finished this manuscript, Southlake made news by electing school board members who strongly opposed the diversity and inclusion training (Hixenbaugh & Hylton, 2021).

2. THE MUTUAL ACCOUNTABILITY MODEL

[1]Portions of this chapter and the next are adapted from a post I wrote for my *Shattering Paradigms* blog on Patheos (Yancey, 2020).

[2]In our book (2010), Michael Emerson and I walk through how this might work in an affirmative action case study.

3. THE REALITY OF INSTITUTIONAL DISCRIMINATION

[1]While I do not want to bring partisan politics too deeply into my analysis, it was clear to me that the election of President Trump was a major catalyst to the radicalization of many people of color. Many had worked with whites for years to foster interracial communication, and they experienced the election of a president who showed little concern about people of color as a slap in the face to that work. It is not a surprise that philosophies such as antiracism became much more popular among people of color after the 2016 presidential election.

4. WHY ANTIRACISM FAILS

[1] I chose not to focus on academic definitions unless they were included in books that were relatively popular since I wanted a definition that was recognizable to non-academics and activists. Debates in academia are not always the debates that are occurring in the general public.

[2] Some may argue that Kendi (2019) has equivalent expectations for whites and nonwhites since he asserts that both can be racist. But Kendi's dichotomy of one being either a racist or antiracist indicates that whites, as well as everyone else, must accept solutions put forth by people of color. Furthermore, Kendi's acceptance of antiracism discrimination is likely to benefit people of color at the expense of whites, but whites are not allowed to assert concerns about that discrimination. Racial minorities can choose to accept a system that one of their own has devised to benefit them, whereas whites must accept his system regardless of the potential cost the system brings to them.

[3] These two studies are not very convincing in their relevance to the general population. Both focus on specialized samples of professionals. The more robust results from metanalyses concerning diversity programs (Lai et al., 2016) and the more expansive sampling in studies connected to the deficiencies of antiracism programs (Cooley et al., 2019; Kidder et al., 2004) remind us of the limitations of those studies.

[4] The demands of antiracists on corporations go beyond mandatory diversity training, employment tests, and grievance committees, but these tactics are more likely to apply to the idea of increasing the number of managers of color. Any other antiracism technique that offers hope for increasing racial diversity among business managers needs to be examined with rigorous empirical testing before we can have confidence in it given the failures documented to date.

5. THE EMPIRICAL BASIS OF MUTUAL ACCOUNTABILITY

[1] The idea behind the job tests is that they would allow people of color to compete with white applicants on an equal basis. The fear was that white managers were using their own social networks to hire other whites who may be their friends. However, the researchers found that white managers would require the tests of applicants of color but not of whites and thus the tests did not turn out to be a useful way to increase people of color in the manager positions.

6. THE THEOLOGICAL BASIS OF MUTUAL ACCOUNTABILITY

[1]When we consider the rich cultural and ethnic diversity of biblical communities, discussions of dealing with intergroup conflict should naturally flow from our Christian tradition. That is why I am grateful for efforts such as Williams (2021), who articulates a biblical theology of kingdom diversity.

[2]This concept of justice is focused on our dealings here on earth. My belief is that God has saved us from ultimate justice, since none of us have earned God's grace. But we are called to do the best we can to provide individuals what they deserve in this life.

7. DOING MUTUAL ACCOUNTABILITY IN OUR LIVES

[1]It is important to note that Byers chose to remain in those multiracial social networks even after facing racism as a black music minister. We have to make choices to remain in multiracial social networks even when people in our racial outgroups let us down.

8. TOWARD A LARGER MOVEMENT OF MUTUAL ACCOUNTABILITY

[1]One such book worth noting is *The Third Option* (McPherson 2020), which states that our common humanity should drive us to conversation with each other. We do not honor that humanity when we either ignore racial identity or shut down dialogue with whites. While I may not agree with everything in the book, I welcome it and any book that moves us beyond the duopoly of colorblindness and antiracism.

[2]For Christians one such resource is the book *Talking About Race* (Adams, 2022), in which the author lays out important yet practical principles for conducting productive conversations. Adams does not take a colorblind or antiracism approach; rather, he provides direction for both whites and nonwhites that is based on producing respect for the racialized other. I highly recommend this book for churches and Christian organizations seeking practical advice on how to engage in collaborative conversations.

[3]I have found that interracial contact may have more power to influence the attitudes of whites in religious settings than in other settings (Yancey, 1999).

[4]This would not be the first time the military has proven to be a place where innovative ideas on racial issues have been tried and been found successful (Butler & Moskos, 1996).

[5]I included the actual name of this individual with his permission since he has blogged on these topics publicly and elsewhere.

[6]Standpoint epistemology is the idea that our experiences affect our knowledge. It is particularly relevant in a critical analysis of racial issues because it indicates that our experience as racialized beings affects what we can and cannot know about reality.

REFERENCES

Adams, I. (2022). *Talking about race: Gospel hope for hard conversations.* Zondervan.

Ajunwa, I. (2020, September 5). 10 reasons why anti-racism training is not the problem. *Forbes.* www.forbes.com/sites/ifeomaajunwa/2020/09/05/10 -reasons-why-anti-racism-training-is-not-the-problem

Alemán Jr., E. (2007). Situating Texas school finance policy in a CRT framework: How "substantially equal" yields racial inequity. *Educational Administration Quarterly, 43*(5), 525-58.

Alhejji, H., Garavan, T., Carbery, R., O'Brien, F., & McGuire, D. (2016). Diversity training programme outcomes: A systematic review. *Human Resource Development Quarterly, 27*(1), 95-149.

Anyaso, H. H. (2020, January 23). Racial discrimination in mortgage market persistent over last few decades. Northwestern. https:// news.northwestern .edu/stories/2020/01/racial-discrimination-in-mortgage-market -persistent-over-last-four-decades

Ascol, T. (2020, February). Critical race theory, intersectionality, and the gospel. Founders Ministries. https://founders.org/2020/02/03 /critical-race-theory-intersectionality-and-the-gospel

Baron, J. (2019, December 11). Traditional diversity training doesn't work. Why not? And what does? Diversity Jobs. www.diversityjobs.com /2019/12/traditional-diversity-training-doesnt-work-why-not-and -what-does

Bartley, N., & Graham, H. D. (2019). *Southern politics and the Second Reconstruction.* JHU Press.

Baumgartner, F. (2016). The Impact of race, gender, and geography on Florida executions. UNC Chapel Hill. https://fbaum.unc.edu/articles /Baumgartner-Florida-executions-Jan2016.pdf

Baumgartner, F. R., Christiani, L., Epp, D. A., Roach, K., & Shoub, K. (2017). Racial disparities in traffic stop outcomes. *Duke Forum for Law & Social Change, 9,* 21-53.

Baumgartner, F. R., Epp, D. A., & Shoub, K. (2018). *Suspect citizens: What 20 million traffic stops tell us about policing and race.* Cambridge University Press.

Bezrukova, K., Spell, C. S., Perry, J. L., & Jehn, K. A. (2016). A meta-analytical integration of over 40 years of research on diversity training evaluation. *Psychological Bulletin, 142*(11), 1227.

Blum, L. (2002). *"I'm not a racist, but . . . ": The moral quandary of race.* Cornell University Press.

Bonilla-Silva, E. (2006). *Racism without racists: Color-blind racism and the persistence of racial inequality in the United States.* Rowman & Littlefield Publishers.

Bonilla-Silva, E. (2020). *Protecting whiteness: Whitelash and the rejection of racial equality.* University of Washington Press.

Brad, L. C. E., Spisz, T. J., & Tanega, C. G. (2019). Does "privilege checking" make us less racist, or more? Generation and political orientation matter. *Race and Social Problems, 11*(1), 1-14.

Brake, T. (2019, May 7). 9 tips for creating more collaborative conversations. TMA World. www.tmaworld.com/our-thinking/9-tips-creating-more -collaborative-conversations

Buckwalter, J. (2008). The transatlantic slave trade and the creation of the English *Weltanschauung,* 1685–1710. Eastern Illinois University. www.eiu .edu/historia/Historia2009Buckwalter.pdf

Bullard, R. D., Johnson, G. S., & Torres, A. O. (2004). *Highway robbery: Transportation racism & new routes to equity.* South End Press.

Butnor, A. (2012). Critical communities: Intellectual safety and the power of disagreement. *Educational Perspectives, 44,* 29-31.

Chapman, S. G. (2012). *The five keys to mindful communication: Using deep listening and mindful speech to strengthen relationships, heal conflicts, and accomplish your goals.* Shambhala Publications.

Christerson, B., Edwards, K. L., & Emerson, M. O. (2005). *Against all odds: The struggle for racial integration in religious organizations.* NYU Press.

Cialdini, R. B. (2001). The science of persuasion. *Scientific American, 284*(2), 76-81.

Cohen, E. G. (1984). The desegregated school: Problems in status power and interethnic climate. In N. Miller & M. B. Brewer, Eds., *Groups in contact* (pp. 77-96). Elsevier.

Combs, B. H. (2016). Black (and brown) bodies out of place: Towards a theoretical understanding of systematic voter suppression in the United States. *Critical Sociology, 42*(4-5), 535-49.

Cooley, E., Brown-Iannuzzi, J. L., Lei, R. F., & Cipolli III, W. (2019). Complex intersections of race and class: Among social liberals, learning about White privilege reduces sympathy, increases blame, and decreases external attributions for White people struggling with poverty. *Journal of Experimental Psychology: General, 148*(12), 2218.

Cooper-White, P. (2012). Denial, victims, and survivors: Post-traumatic identity formation and monuments in heaven. *Journal of Pastoral Theology, 22*(1), 2-1–2-16.

Cox, J. M. (2009). Frequent arrests, harsh sentencing, and the disproportionate impact they have on African Americans and their community. *S. Region Black Students Ass'n LJ, 3*, 17.

Deutsch, M., & Collins, M. E. (1951). *Interracial housing: A psychological evaluation of a social experiment.* University of Minnesota Press.

DiAngelo, R. (2018). *White fragility: Why it's so hard for white people to talk about racism.* Beacon Press.

Dobbin, F., & Kalev, A. (2016, July–August). Why diversity programs fail. *Harvard Business Review.* https://hbr.org/2016/07/why-diversity-programs-fail

Dover, T. L., Kaiser, C. R., & Major, B. (2020). Mixed signals: The unintended effects of diversity initiatives. *Social Issues and Policy Review, 14*(1), 152-81.

Duguid, M. M., & Thomas-Hunt, M. C. (2015). Condoning stereotyping? How awareness of stereotyping prevalence impacts expression of stereotypes. *Journal of Applied Psychology, 100*(2), 343.

Eddo-Lodge, R. (2020). *Why I'm no longer talking to white people about race.* Bloomsbury Publishing.

Ellis, D., & Fisher, B. (1994). *Small group decision making: Communication and the group process.* McGrath-Hill.

Emerson, M. O. (2010). *People of the dream: Multiracial congregations in the United States.* Princeton University Press.

Emerson, M. O., & Yancey, G. (2010). *Transcending racial barriers: Toward a mutual obligations approach.* Oxford University Press.

English, M., & Kalla, J. (2021). Racial equality frames and public policy support: Survey experimental evidence. https://doi.org/10.31219/osf.io/tdkf3

Fausel, D. F. (1998). Collaborative conversations for change: A solution focused approach to family centered practice. *Journal of Family Strengths, 3*(1), 7.

Fidel, K. (2020). *The antiracist: How to start the conversation about race and take action.* Hot Books.

Fisher, A. L. (2020, August 12). Wanting to fire people for supporting Trump or Biden is cancel culture. Insider. www.businessinsider.com /cancel-culture-firing-people-donating-major-party-candidate-trump -biden-2020-8

Fox, A., & Thomas, T. (2008). Impact of religious affiliation and religiosity on forgiveness. *Australian Psychologist, 43*(3), 175-85.

Free, M. D. (1996). *African Americans and the criminal justice system: Vol. 13.* Taylor & Francis.

Gaertner, S. L., Dovidio, J. F., & Bachman, B. A. (1996). Revisiting the contact hypothesis: The induction of a common ingroup identity. *International Journal of Intercultural Relations, 20*(3-4), 271-90.

Gallagher, C. A. (2003). Color-blind privilege: The social and political functions of erasing the color line in post race America. *Race, Gender & Class, 10*(4), 22-37.

Geran Pilon, J. (2020). 2020 America and the cancel culture of fools. *Israel Journal of Foreign Affairs, 14*(2), 183-96.

Golub, A., Marcantonio, R. A., & Sanchez, T. W. (2013). Race, space, and struggles for mobility: Transportation impacts on African Americans in Oakland and the East Bay. *Urban Geography, 34*(5), 699-728.

Gross, S., Possley, M., & Stephens, K. (2017). *Race and wrongful convictions in the United States.* University of California, Irvine. www.law.umich .edu/special/exoneration/Documents/Race_and_Wrongful_Convictions .pdf

Guh, J., Harris, C., Martinez, P., Chen, F., & Gianutsos, L. P. (2019). Antiracism in residency: A multimethod intervention to increase racial diversity in a community-based residency program. *Family Medicine, 51*(1), 37-40.

Harris, D. A. (1999). The stories, the statistics, and the law: Why driving while black matters. University of Minnesota Law School Scholarship Repository. https://scholarship.law.umn.edu/cgi/viewcontent.cgi ?article=2132&context=mlr

Heilman, M. E., & Welle, B. (2006). Disadvantaged by diversity? The effects of diversity goals on competence perceptions 1. *Journal of Applied Social Psychology, 36*(5), 1291-319.

Hixenbaugh, M. (2021, January 22). A viral video forced a wealthy Texas suburb to confront racism. A 'silent majority' fought back. NBC News. www.nbcnews.com/news/us-news/viral-video-forced-wealthy-texas -suburb-confront-racism-silent-majority-n1255230

Hixenbaugh, M., & Hylton, A. (2021, May 2). In bitterly divided election in Southlake, Texas, opponents of anti-racism education win big. NBC News. www.nbcnews.com/news/us-news/bitterly-divided-election -southlake-texas-opponents-anti-racism-education-win-n1266102

Hoffower, H. (2020, June 8). What it really means to be an anti-racist, and why it's not the same as being an ally. Insider. www.businessinsider.com /what-is-anti-racism-how-to-be-anti-racist-2020-6

Holcomb, J. E., Williams, M. R., & Demuth, S. (2004). White female victims and death penalty disparity research. *Justice Quarterly, 21*(4), 877-902.

Hong, L., & Page, S. E. (2004). Groups of diverse problem solvers can outperform groups of high-ability problem solvers. *Proceedings of the National Academy of Sciences, 101*(46), 16385-9.

Howell, J., & Emerson, M. O. (2018). Preserving racial hierarchy amidst changing racial demographics: How neighbourhood racial preferences are changing while maintaining segregation. *Ethnic and Racial Studies, 41*(15), 2770-89.

Hughes, C. (2019, January 17). Martin Luther King, colorblind radical. *Wall Street Journal.* www.wsj.com/articles/martin-luther-king-colorblind -radical-11547769741

Jackson, A. (2016, July 28). 'Disinvitations' for college speakers are on the rise— here's a list of people turned away this year. Insider. www.businessinsider .com/list-of-disinvited-speakers-at-colleges-2016-7

Jewell, T. (2020). *This book is anti-racist.* London: Frances Lincoln.

Johnson, L. M., Antle, B. F., & Barbee, A. P. (2009). Addressing dispropor- tionality and disparity in child welfare: Evaluation of an anti-racism training for community service providers. *Children and Youth Services Review, 31*(6), 688-96.

Jost, M., Whitfield, E. L., & Jost, M. (2005). When the rules are fair, but the game isn't. *Multicultural Education, 13*(1), 14.

Judkis, M. (2020, July 8). Anti-racism trainers were ready for this moment. Is everyone else? *Washington Post.* www.washingtonpost.com/lifestyle /style/anti-racism-trainers-were-ready-for-this-moment-is-everyone

-else/2020/07/07/df2d39ea-b582-11ea-a510-55bf26485c93
_story.html

Kaiser, C. R., Major, B., Jurcevic, I., Dover, T. L., Brady, L. M., & Shapiro, J. R. (2013). Presumed fair: Ironic effects of organizational diversity structures. *Journal of Personality and Social Psychology, 104*(3), 504.

Katz, P. A., & Taylor, D. A. (2013). *Eliminating racism: Profiles in controversy.* Springer Science & Business Media.

Keller, T. (2020). The sin of racism. Life in the Gospel. https://quarterly .gospelinlife.com/the-sin-of-racism

Kendall, M. (2021). *Hood feminism: Notes from the women that a movement forgot.* Penguin.

Kendi, I. X. (2019). *How to be an antiracist.* One World.

Kidder, D. L., Lankau, M. J., Chrobot-Mason, D., Mollica, K. A., & Friedman, R. A. (2004). Backlash toward diversity initiatives: Examining the impact of diversity program justification, personal and group outcomes. *International Journal of Conflict Management, 15*(1), 77-102.

Kim, Y. (2015). Does disagreement mitigate polarization? How selective exposure and disagreement affect political polarization. *Journalism & Mass Communication Quarterly, 92*(4), 915-37.

King, M. L., Jr. (1962, October 15). An address by the Reverend Dr. Martin Luther King Jr. Cornell College. https://news.cornellcollege.edu/dr -martin-luther-kings-visit-to-cornell-college

Kivel, P. (2017). *Uprooting racism: How white people can work for racial justice.* New Society Publishers.

Knight, J. (1991, October 22). Race factor in mortgage lending seen. *Washington Post.*

Krysan, M., Couper, M. P., Farley, R., & Forman, T. A. (2009). Does race matter in neighborhood preferences? Results from a video experiment. *American Journal of Sociology, 115*(2), 527-59.

Krysan, M., & Farley, R. (2002). The residential preferences of blacks: Do they explain persistent segregation? *Social Forces, 80*(3), 937-80.

Lai, C. K., Skinner, A. L., Cooley, E., Murrar, S., Brauer, M., Devos, T., . . . Marshburn, C. K. (2016). Reducing implicit racial preferences: II. Intervention effectiveness across time. *Journal of Experimental Psychology: General, 145*(8), 1001.

Legault, L., Gutsell, J. N., & Inzlicht, M. (2011). Ironic effects of antiprej-udice messages: How motivational interventions can reduce (but also increase) prejudice. *Psychological Science, 22*(12), 1472-7.

Lerman, A. E., & Acland, D. (2020). United in states of dissatisfaction: Confirmation bias across the partisan divide. *American Politics Research,* *48*(2), 227-37.

Lindsey, A., King, E., Hebl, M., & Levine, N. (2015). The impact of method, motivation, and empathy on diversity training effectiveness. *Journal of Business and Psychology, 30*(3), 605-17.

Lurigio, A. J., & Loose, P. (2008). The disproportionate incarceration of African Americans for drug offenses: The national and Illinois perspective. *Journal of Ethnicity in Criminal Justice, 6*(3), 223-47.

Mac Donald, H. (2018). *The diversity delusion: How race and gender pandering corrupt the university and undermine our culture.* St. Martin's Press.

MacPherson, S. (2010). Teachers' collaborative conversations about culture: Negotiating decision making in intercultural teaching. *Journal of Teacher Education, 61*(3), 271-86.

Manning, A. (2020, December 1). Stand firm against critical race theory. Church Acadiana. http://churchacadiana.com/wp-content/uploads/2020/12/STAND-FIRM-AGAINST-CRITICAL-RACE-THEORY-1.pdf

Mannix, E., & Neale, M. A. (2005). What differences make a difference? The promise and reality of diverse teams in organizations. *Psychological Science in the Public Interest, 6*(2), 31-55.

Maples, J. (2019, June 12). Southern Baptist Convention to officially affirm Marxist critical theory as viable. Reformation Charlotte. https://reformationcharlotte.org/2019/06/12/southern-baptist-convention-officially-affirms-marxist-critical-theory-as-viable

Marable, M. (1984). *Race, reform and rebellion: The Second Reconstruction in black America, 1945–1982.* Macmillan International Higher Education.

Massey, D., & Denton, N. A. (1993). *American apartheid: Segregation and the making of the underclass.* Harvard University Press.

May, S. (2007). *How to argue so your spouse will listen: 6 principles for turning arguments into conversations.* Thomas Nelson.

McNamee, L. G. (2011). Faith-based organizational communication and its implications for member identity. *Journal of Applied Communication Research, 39*(4), 422-40.

McWhorter, J. H. (2009, September 23). Colour-Blind. Manhattan Institute. www.manhattan-institute.org/html/colour-blind-2019.html

Miller, A. (2002). *The truth will set you free: Overcoming emotional blindness and finding your true adult self.* Basic Books.

Mitchell, O. (2005). A meta-analysis of race and sentencing research: Explaining the inconsistencies. *Journal of Quantitative Criminology, 21*(4), 439-66.

Mohr, J. J., Fisher, R. J., & Nevin, J. R. (1996). Collaborative communication in interfirm relationships: Moderating effects of integration and control. *Journal of Marketing, 60*(3), 103-15.

Mutz, D. C. (2006). *Hearing the other side: Deliberative versus participatory democracy.* Cambridge University Press.

Neville, H. A., Gallardo, M. E., & Sue, D. W. E. (2016). *The myth of racial color blindness: Manifestations, dynamics, and impact.* American Psychological Association.

Nickerson, R. S. (1998). Confirmation bias: A ubiquitous phenomenon in many guises. *Review of General Psychology, 2*(2), 175-220.

O'Brien, L. T., & Major, B. (2005). System-justifying beliefs and psychological well-being: The roles of group status and identity. *Personality and Social Psychology Bulletin, 31*(12), 1718-29.

O'Flaherty, B., & Sethi, R. (2010). Homicide in black and white. *Journal of Urban Economics, 68*(3), 215-30.

Oluo, I. (2019). *So you want to talk about race.* Hachette UK.

Paluck, E. L., & Green, D. P. (2009). Prejudice reduction: What works? A review and assessment of research and practice. *Annual Review of Psychology, 60*, 339-67.

Pan, J. C. (2020, January 7). Why diversity training isn't enough. The New Republic. https://newrepublic.com/article/156032/diversity-training -isnt-enough-pamela-newkirk-robin-diangelo-books-reviews

Paradies, Y., Truong, M., & Priest, N. (2014). A systematic review of the extent and measurement of healthcare provider racism. *Journal of General Internal Medicine, 29*(2), 364-87.

Paulus, T. M. (2006). Challenge or connect? Dialogue in online learning environments. *Journal of Computing in Higher Education, 18*(1), 3.

Peacock, B. (2020, June 10). The evangelical church's confused witness on race: Part 2. Excellent Thought. www.excellentthought.net/the -evangelical-churchs-confused-witness-on-race-part-2

Peffley, M., & Hurwitz, J. (2010). *Justice in America: The separate realities of Blacks and Whites.* Cambridge University Press.

Perkins, S., & Rice, C. (2000). *More than equals: Racial healing for the sake of the gospel.* InterVarsity Press.

Perry, R. (2007). *"Race" and racism: The development of modern racism in America.* Springer.

Pettigrew, T. F., & Tropp, L. R. (2006). A meta-analytic test of intergroup contact theory. *Journal of Personality and Social Psychology, 90*(5), 751.

Plant, E. A., & Devine, P. G. (2001). Responses to other-imposed pro-Black pressure: Acceptance or backlash? *Journal of Experimental Social Psychology, 37*(6), 486-501.

Polletta, F., & Maresca, A. (2021). Claiming Martin Luther King, Jr. for the right: The Martin Luther King Day holiday in the Reagan era. *Memory Studies,* https://doi.org/10.1177/1750698021995932.

Pollock, M. (2008). *Everyday antiracism: Getting real about race in school.* The New Press.

Prather, C., Fuller, T. R., Marshall, K. J., & Jeffries IV, W. L. (2016). The impact of racism on the sexual and reproductive health of African American women. *Journal of Women's Health, 25*(7), 664-71.

Quillian, L. (2002). Why is black-white residential segregation so persistent? Evidence on three theories from migration data. *Social Science Research, 31*(2), 197-229.

Quillian, L. (2014). Does segregation create winners and losers? Residential segregation and inequality in educational attainment. *Social Problems, 61*(3), 402-26.

Quillian, L., Pager, D., Hexel, O., & Midtbøen, A. H. (2017). Meta-analysis of field experiments shows no change in racial discrimination in hiring over time. *Proceedings of the National Academy of Sciences, 114*(41), 10870-75.

Roberts, J. (2016). Race and the origins of plantation slavery. *Oxford Research Encyclopedia of American History.* https://oxfordre.com/americanhistory/view/10.1093/acrefore/9780199329175.001.0001/acrefore-978019 9329175-e-268

Saad, L. F. (2020). *Me and white supremacy: Combat racism, change the world, and become a good ancestor.* Sourcebooks.

Sanchez, J. I., & Medkik, N. (2004). The effects of diversity awareness training on differential treatment. *Group & Organization Management, 29*(4), 517-36.

Santoro, W. A. (2015). Was the civil rights movement successful? Tracking and understanding black views. *Sociological Forum, 30*(S1), 627-47.

Schuman, H., Steeh, C., Bobo, L., & Krysan, M. (1997). *Racial attitudes in America: Trends and interpretations.* Harvard University Press.

Shapiro, T., Meschede, T., & Osoro, S. (2013). The roots of the widening racial wealth gap: Explaining the black-white economic divide. Institute on Assets and Social Policy. https://heller.brandeis.edu/iere/pdfs /racial-wealth-equity/racial-wealth-gap/roots-widening-racial-wealth -gap.pdf

Sikkink, D., & Emerson, M. O. (2008). School choice and racial segregation in US schools: The role of parents' education. *Ethnic and Racial Studies, 31*(2), 267-93.

Slocum, F., & Lee, Y.-T. (2004). Racism, racial stereotypes and American politics. In J. L. Chin, Ed., *Psychology of Prejudice and Discrimination: Vol. 1* (pp. 61-93). Praeger Perspectives.

Snyder, I. (2020, July 21). What does it mean to be an anti-racist? National League of Cities. www.nlc.org/article/2020/07/21/what-does-it-mean -to-be-an-anti-racist

Soave, R. (2020, August 14). UConn will pay *White Fragility* author Robin DiAngelo $20,000 to train school administrators. Reason. https:// reason.com/2020/08/14/uconn-will-pay-white-fragility-author -robin-diangelo-20000-to-train-school-administrators

Speaker Booking Agency. (2020). Tim Wise speaker & booking information. www.speakerbookingagency.com/talent/tim-wise

St. John, N. H. (1975). *School desegregation: Outcomes for children*. Wiley.

Sunstein, C. R., & Hastie, R. (2015). *Wiser: Getting beyond groupthink to make groups smarter*. Harvard Business Press.

Tomkin, A. R. (2020, December 14). Unpacking the false allyship of white racial justice leaders. NPQ. https://nonprofitquarterly.org/unpacking -the-false-allyship-of-white-racial-justice-leaders

Turner, R. (1996). The dangers of misappropriation: Misusing Martin Luther King, Jr.'s legacy to prove the colorblind thesis. *Michigan Journal of Race & Law, 2*, 101.

Walters, P. B. (2001). Educational access and the state: Historical continuities and discontinuities in racial inequality in American education. *Sociology of Education, 74*, 35-49.

Watkins, M. (2001). In practice: Principles of persuasion. *Negotiation Journal, 17*(2), 115-37.

Williams, J. J. (2021). *Redemptive kingdom diversity: A biblical theology of the people of God*. Baker Academic.

Wilson, T. E. J. (2017, July). A black man goes undercover in the alt-right. TED. www.ted.com/talks/theo_e_j_wilson_a_black_man_goes_undercover _in_the_alt_right

Winnubst, S. (2020). The ontological crisis of the "human." In M. M. Shew & K. K. Garchar (Eds.), *Philosophy for girls: An invitation to the life of thought* (pp. 181-92). Oxford University Press.

Wolfelt, A. D. (2004). *Understanding your grief: Ten essential touchstones for finding hope and healing your heart.* Companion Press.

Yancey, G. (1999). An examination of the effects of residential and church integration on racial attitudes of whites. *Sociological Perspectives, 42*(2), 279-304.

Yancey, G. (2005). "Blacks cannot be racists": A look at how European-Americans, African-Americans, Hispanic-Americans and Asian-Americans perceive minority racism. *Michigan Sociological Review, 19*(Fall), 138-54.

Yancey, G. (2006). *Beyond racial gridlock: Embracing mutual responsibility.* InterVarsity Press.

Yancey, G. (2007). *Interracial contact and social change.* Lynne Rienner Publishers.

Yancey, G. (2010). *Neither Jew nor Gentile: Exploring issues of racial diversity on Protestant college campuses.* Oxford University Press.

Yancey, G., Hubbard, E., & Smith, A. (2009). Unequally yoked: How willing are Christians to engage in interracial and interfaith dating? In E. Smith & A. Hattery (Eds.), *Interracial Relationships in the 21st Century.* Carolina Academic Press.

Yancey, G. (2020, August 19). Why we cannot ignore Institutional Racism. *Shattering Paradigms,* Patheos. www.patheos.com/blogs/shatteringpara digms/2020/08/why-we-cannot-ignore-institutional-racism

Yancey, G., & Quosigk, A. R. (2021). *One faith no longer: The transformation of Christianity in red and blue America.* New York University Press.

Yancey, G., & Williamson, D. (2012). *What motivates cultural progressives: Understanding opposition to the political and Christian right.* Baylor University Press.

Yanco, J. J. (2014). *Misremembering Dr. King: Revisiting the legacy of Martin Luther King Jr.* Indiana University Press.

Yi, J., Todd, N. R., & Mekawi, Y. (2020). Racial colorblindness and confidence in and likelihood of action to address prejudice. *American Journal of Community Psychology, 65*(3-4), 407-22.

Zuckerman, E. (2011). EEOC politics and limits on Reagan's civil rights legacy. In D. McGuire & J. Dittmer (Eds.), *Freedom Rights: New Perspectives on the Civil Rights Movement* (pp. 247-75). University Press of Kentucky.

ALSO BY
GEORGE YANCEY

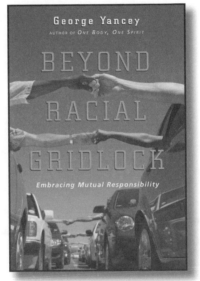

Beyond Racial Gridlock
978-0-8308-3376-4